THE Bible TO Life

THE Bible TO Life

Making Biblical Truth Memorable

TERRENCE W. SMITH

XULON ELITE

Xulon Press Elite
555 Winderley Pl, Suite 225
Maitland, FL 32751
407.339.4217
www.xulonpress.com

Paperback ISBN-13: 979-8-86850-075-6
Ebook ISBN-13: 979-8-86850-076-3

Contents

Introduction

The Bible to Life, Making Biblical Truth Memorable, is a hopeful and expectant attempt to bring to the surface the amazing truth of God's word in a way that will burn into reader's memories and lives. The desperate need for wisdom from the Bible and application of its teachings is probably more important today than ever before and can result in one's growing relationship with God the Father! The apostle Peter encouraged believers to strongly desire God's word; "Like newborn babies, crave pure spiritual milk, so that by it you might grow up in your salvation." (1 Peter 2:2) Add to this the challenge from Jesus' half brother James to be actively involved in spiritual growth, "Do not merely listen to the word... do what it says." (James 1:22)

Memory aids (mnemonics[1]) like acronyms and acrostics are used to make the topics memorable and more applicable (if you can't remember something, how will you be able to apply it?). The Bible is understood and used as the standard text for truth in this writing, since it is God's words to mankind. Also, pronouns for God, Jesus and the Holy Spirit are capitalized as in some of the best Bible translations[2] to help with context and

---

[1] Definition of mnemonic: "1. assisting or intended to assist memory. To distinguish 'principal' from 'principle' use the mnemonic aid 'the principal is your pal'. 2. of or relating to memory mnemonic skill." https://www.merriam-webster.com/dictionary/mnemonic.

[2] The New American Standard, Holman Christian Standard and the Legacy Standard Bibles.

to honor and respect God's holiness[3] and sovereignty (authority).[4] Several Bible translations are used, but the one used most and not labeled is the New International Version 1984 edition because it is easy to read and understand, accurate, and offers a generous copy policy for publishing (but it does not capitalize pronouns for the Trinity as I do).

May God bring ***The Bible to Life*** in your life as you read and reflect on this book!

> *I shall delight in Your statutes; **I shall not forget Your word**. (Psalms 119:16, NASB)*

> *So I will always **remind you** of these things, even though you know them and are firmly established in the truth you now have. I think it is right to **refresh your memory** as long as I live in the tent of this body, because I know that I will soon put it aside, as our Lord Jesus Christ has made clear to me. And I will make every effort to see that after my departure you will always be able to **remember** these things. (2 Peter 1:12-15)*

---

[3] Holiness means "sacred, blameless" according to Strong's Talking Greek and Hebrew Dictionary (Strong's Dictionary), #40.

[4] Sovereignty is defined as "supreme power... freedom from external control... autonomy" by Merriam-Webster.com. Dictionary.com defines it as "having supreme power or authority, controlling influence."

The Bible to Life

Chapter 1

It's as Simple as ABC...

Admit sin,
Believe in Jesus Christ, and
Confess Jesus is Lord.

Admit

In the second year of my bachelor's degree, I transferred to a small Bible college where after a little while I thought I knew everyone. But a friend noted that we had a few "phantom" students floating around. They were the ones who we only caught a glimpse of on rare occasions, and we would ask each other who they were. Of course they were not really ghosts, but quiet, reserved students who probably just spent their time mostly in the library or their dorm rooms studying (who would have thought of such a thing?). Sin has become just as elusive to us in our modern culture. We don't see it in ourselves, and we don't admit it if we do. After-all, something is only sinful if we feel it is wrong or if someone else does something we don't like, right? We are all basically good, right? Wrong! The Bible says, "If we claim to be without sin, we deceive ourselves and the truth is not in us." (1 John 1:8) Jesus even said, "no one is good, except God alone." (Luke 18:19b)[5]

---

[5] "As it is written: "There is no one righteous, not even one; 11 there is no one who understands, no one who seeks God. 12 All have turned away, they have together become worthless; there is no one who does good, not even one." Romans 3:10-12.

Sin is universal; "all have sinned and fall short of God's glory..." (Romans 3:23). I checked the "all" in the original language this verse was written in (Greek) and it means "all, everyone."[6] You and I and everyone else has fallen short of God's standard, and needs forgiveness and cleansing that only God can give, but there is more. Note that in the famous John 3:16 verse Jesus gave His life so that we would not "perish" but have eternal life. The word "perish" means to be "utterly destroyed"[7]. Why will people perish? The Bible tells us it is because of sin, "The wages of sin is death..." (Romans 6:23), and it is a barrier between God and man that must be removed; "If I had cherished sin in my heart, the Lord would not have listened." (Psalms 66:18). That is why Jesus died on the cross, to pay the penalty of sin and make a bridge to God. He alone could span the gap between us and Him since He was fully God and fully man![8]

The path forward is to **admit** our sins to Him. Then He will forgive us and "cleans us from all unrighteousness." (1 John 1:9, see verse 8 also) Our sins will be removed from us "as far as the east is from the west" (Psalm 103:12) and God told His people a long time ago that He would even forget their sins, "I, even I, am He who blots out your transgressions, for My own

---

[6] All = *pas*, #3956. New American Standard Exhaustive Concordance of the Bible (NASB Concordance).

[7] Perish = *apollumi*, #622. Ibid.

[8] Philippians 2:7-8, "but (Jesus Christ) made himself nothing, taking the very nature of a servant, being made in human likeness. And being found in appearance as a man, he humbled himself and became obedient to death— even death on a cross!" John 1:1-3, "In the beginning was the Word, and the Word was with God, and the Word was God. He was with God in the beginning. Through him all things were made; without him nothing was made that has been made." John 1:14, "The Word became flesh and made his dwelling among us. We have seen his glory, the glory of the One and Only, who came from the Father, full of grace and truth."

sake, and remembers your sins no more." (Isaiah 43:25) God is willing to cleanse, forgive, and even forget our sin, what a great God! Have you admitted your sin to Him?

Believe

Growth begins with birth. It is a simple truth, yet one that is often ignored. We are not just born to mature physically, intellectually, socially and emotionally—but spiritually. The Bible says we are body and spirit (James 2:26) For someone to follow Jesus and grow in a relationship with Him, they must understand that spiritual life begins with spiritual birth. That is what Jesus told Nicodemus in John's Gospel, "You must be born again." (3:7) In fact, previous to that statement He said, "... no one can see the kingdom of God unless he is born again." Being born spiritually is a requirement to growing in and following Jesus!

You might ask "How can I be born again?" Jesus gave the answer in verse 16 where He said "Whoever **believes** in Him (Jesus) shall not perish but have eternal life." Belief is primary, and in the Bible it normally means "trust, to entrust"[9]. To entrust someone means "to commit to another with confidence".[10] We must entrust ourselves or commit to Jesus with confidence in His grace, sacrifice and love. He alone can save us. He alone truly loves us. This kind of belief kick-starts our relationship with God.

Confess

When Paul wrote to the church in Rome, he knew he was communicating with people who were steeped in a culture that believed in a number of gods and that the emperor himself

---

[9] Faith = *pisteuo*, #4100. NASB Concordance.

[10] https://www.merriam-webster.com/dictionary/entrust

was often worshiped or demanded to be worshiped as a god. While our gods are different today, we still have them. A god can be anything that we place above Jesus Christ in our lives, such as addictive substances (alcohol, drugs), money, people, careers, etc.

Paul made it very clear that Jesus Christ must be believed (trusted) to be their God; "... if you **confess** with your mouth, 'Jesus is Lord,' and believe in your heart that God raised him from the dead, you will be saved. 10 For it is with your heart that you believe and are justified, and it is with your mouth that you confess and are saved." (Rom 10:9-10) The word "confess" means "to speak the same, to agree" and literally means "to be of the same mind"[11], and the word "Lord" also means "master, owner."[12] Paul is clearly encouraging us to know that God wants us to be of the same mind with Him concerning Jesus being our Master and Owner! When we come to this point of confession and submission regarding Jesus, we truly will be "saved" and made new.[13]

ABC:

Admit sin,
Believe in Jesus Christ, and
Confess Jesus is Lord.

---

[11] Confess = *homologeo*, #3670. NASB Concordance.

[12] Lord = *kurios*, #2692. NASB Concordance.

[13] "Therefore, if anyone is in Christ, he is a new creation; the old has gone, the new has come!" 2 Corinthians 5:17.

Growing Deeper...

▶ Have you **A**dmitted your sin, **B**elieved in Jesus Christ and **C**onfessed Him as Lord? If you have not, take time right now to get things settled with God!

▶ Find a Bible believing and teaching church[14] to become part of. You will be glad you did.

---

[14] Most Bible believing churches are called evangelical churches, which is a reference to evangelism or sharing the gospel or "good news" about Jesus Christ with others. Other terms that may be used for Bible believing churches are conservative and fundamental, with each being a little more strict regarding their beliefs and practices.

The Bible to Life

Chapter 2

ACT on Sin

Acknowledge,
Confess, and
Turn from it.

I remember the first time I used a switch (which in the old days was a small slender flexible stick) to punish my second son Matt for directly disobeying his mom and I. Remembering Proverbs 13:24 which states "He who spares the rod hates his son, but he who loves him is careful to discipline him." On this particular occasion, we saw no other recourse but to spank his bare backside with the "rod" a couple times. Of course he cried profusely and broke our hearts. Spanking him was one of the most difficult things for me to do as a parent, but it was successful. A few minutes after he had settled down, Matt came to me and said these shocking and unforgettable words, "Daddy, I love you." He somehow knew he had disobeyed and the resulting discipline showed him he was loved!

After the prophet Nathan came to King David to confront him over his adultery with Bathsheba, David also expressed his remorse and love to his heavenly Father when he wrote Psalm 51. Here we find in the first 13 verses how we should **ACT** on our sin as he did:

1 Have mercy on me, O God, according to your unfailing love; according to your great compassion blot out my transgressions.

2 Wash away all my iniquity and cleanse me from my sin.

3 For **I know my transgressions, and my sin is always before me.**

4 **Against you, you only, have I sinned** and done what is evil in your sight, so that you are proved right when you speak and justified when you judge.

5 Surely I was sinful at birth, sinful from the time my mother conceived me.

6 Surely you desire truth in the inner parts; you teach me wisdom in the inmost place.

7 Cleanse me with hyssop, and I will be clean; wash me, and I will be whiter than snow.

8 Let me hear joy and gladness; let the bones you have crushed rejoice.

9 Hide your face from my sins and blot out all my iniquity.

10 Create in me a pure heart, O God, and renew a steadfast spirit within me.

11 Do not cast me from your presence or take your Holy Spirit from me.

12 Restore to me the joy of your salvation and grant me a willing spirit, to sustain me.

13 Then I will teach transgressors your ways, and sinners will **turn back to you**.

Acknowledge

Note in verse 3 that David **acknowledged** his sin to God when he confessed, "I know my transgressions…" Nathan challenged David on his sinful act with Bethsheba and David honestly and immediately recognized his sin. This should not be that difficult of a step for us to make either, since "....all have sinned and fall short of the glory of God." (Romans 3:23) The Apostle John also wrote in a parallel New Testament passage, "If we claim to be without sin, we deceive ourselves and the truth is not in us." (1 John 1:8) Taking the first step towards freedom means being honest with God by acknowledging our sin to Him.

Confess

Verse 4 reveals that David **confessed** his sin toward God as well, "Against you only have I sinned…" Again, the Apostle John encouraged this next action when He wrote, "If we confess our sins, he is faithful and just and will forgive us our sins and purify us from all unrighteousness." (1 John 1:9) The forgiveness and purification God promises is well worth the acknowledgment and confession we need to make!

Turn

Then David took what may be the most difficult step, he **turned** from his sin. We see this disclosed in verses 10-13 where he pens these profound and memorable words, "Create in me a pure heart, O God, and renew a steadfast spirit within me." (NASB) Then a few lines later he adds, "...sinners will turn back to you." John again agrees;

> We know that we have come to know him if we obey his commands. The man who says, "I know him," but does not do what he commands is a liar, and the truth is not in him. But if anyone obeys his word, God's love is truly made complete in him. This is how we know we are in him: Whoever claims to live in him must walk as Jesus did. (1 John 2:3-6)

To turn from sin is repentance. In Matthew 3:2 John the Baptist calls out for the people to repent; "Repent, for the kingdom of heaven is at hand." The word "repent" means to "change one's mind... change the way you perceive or think."[15] Once someone changes his or her mind about sin, it should result in changed behavior as it did in David's life, and there should be a passion to please and serve God, as 2 Corinthians 5:17 confirms; "Therefore if anyone is in Christ, *he is* a new creature; the old things passed away; behold, new things have come." (NASB) And to Timothy, Paul wrote,

> Here is a trustworthy saying that deserves full acceptance: Christ Jesus came into the world to save sinners—of whom I am the worst. But for that very reason I was shown mercy so that in me, the worst of sinners, Christ Jesus might display his unlimited patience as an example for those who would believe on him and receive eternal life. (1 Timothy 1:15-16)

ACT on sin:

Acknowledge,
Confess, and
Turn from it.

---

[15] Repent = to change one's mind, μετανοέω, metanoeô, 3340. Root: from 3326 and 3539; 3539 νοέω, noeô = "to perceive, think." NASB Concordance.

Growing Deeper...

▶ Do you have any sin you need to **ACT** on?

▶ Is there sin in your life that you have **Acknowledged** and **Confessed** that you have not yet **Turned** from?

▶ What is keeping you from turning away from sin and walking freely with your heavenly Father?

▶ Why not start now?

The Bible to Life

Chapter 3

The FADE Into Sin

Foolish,
Antagonistic,
Deceived, and
Enslaved.

The Bible tells us that there are four consecutive steps that people take when they unwittingly slide into slavery to sin. Titus 3:3 reveals this truth this way, "At one time we too were **foolish, disobedient, deceived** and **enslaved** by all kinds of passions and pleasures. We lived in malice and envy, being hated and hating one another."

Paul reminds Titus that they both were foolish as well earlier in their lives, and that people are naturally led into disobedience, deception and enslavement. The undesired results are malice, hatred and envy. A useful acronym to help us better understand and remember these four slippery steps toward addictive sin is the word **FADE**.

Foolish

The first word that Paul uses in his discussion is the word **foolish**. The word foolish is defined here in Greek as "not understanding, unwise"[16] and some synonyms are, "brainless, daft, inept, loony, kooky, mad, and nonsensical." Everyone likes to fool around a little bit or a lot and if we are too foolish in our behavior we may become the ones characterized as brainless or mad.

Antagonistic

If we continue living foolishly we are in danger of becoming disobedient and even **antagonistic** towards those in authority over us, or more importantly, towards God. This rebelliousness starts out small, but the more foolish we are, the more wayward and antagonistic we will likely become.

Deceived

The buildup continues as the antagonistic attitude and behavior leads us into being **deceived**. When we are deceived we are incapable of seeing the truth of our own situation. Harm that is done to others around us is invisible to our own thoughts and senses. We begin to believe things that we never would have conceived of before we became so rebellious towards God.

I remember on more than one occasion trying to have a conversation with my dad when he was falling-down drunk, hardly able to stand or think and touting out contradictory statements like, "I am not drunk! I am just as sober as anyone else!" Even when he was sober, he would not admit to being an alcoholic or hopelessly addicted. Obviously he was blind to his own condition as so many substance abusers are.

---

[16] Foolish = "not understanding, unwise", ἀνόητος (anoêtos), 453. NASB Concordance.

Enslaved

In this deceived state, one becomes **enslaved** in sin and will never get out of such a dark prison on his own strength. There is nothing he can do to break free on his own. There is only One hero who can set us free from our chains and that is Jesus Christ Himself! Jesus preached, "So if the Son sets you free, you will be free indeed." (John 8:36) The letter to the Corinthian church (2 Corinthians 5:17) adds that we are not only free, we are by God's grace made "new"; "Therefore, if anyone is in Christ, the new creation has come: The old has gone, the new is here!"

By the way, my dad came to Christ about three years before he passed away. During that time he read his Bible, did not drink a drop of booze and completely quit chain smoking. Only Jesus Christ can make such a drastic and lasting change like that in someone's life!

Only Jesus Christ can make such a drastic and lasting change...

The FADE into Sin:

Foolish,
Antagonistic,
Deceived, and
Enslaved.

Growing Deeper...

▶ Be honest with yourself and ask if you are in one of these steps right now? Which one?

▶ What do you plan to do about it?

▶ Find a Godly person like a pastor or elder or other leader of a church who knows Jesus Christ and the Bible well and loves people. Ask for prayer and help. Don't be afraid to ask since they were once enslaved in some way too!

The Bible to Life

Chapter 4

FEAR of God,
Remedy for Temptation

Fear and Love God,
Escape from What Tempts You,
Apply Scripture, and
Remain Faithful to Christ.

L et's begin our query on the subject of temptation with an elementary question, what is it? In the Greek New Testament, temptation is defined as "an experiment, a trial, a solicitation, by implication, adversity."[17] James 1:12-15 uses the term 6 times and provides deeper meaning and understanding of its implications;

> Blessed is the man who perseveres under trial (temptation), because when he has stood the test, he will receive the crown of life that God has promised to those who love him. 13 When tempted, no one should say, "God is tempting me." For God cannot be tempted by evil, nor does he tempt anyone; 14 but each one is tempted when, by his own evil desire, he is dragged away and enticed.

---

[17] Trial/tempted/tempt = "an experiment, a trial, temptation." πειρασμός (pi-ras-mos'). (NASB Concordance) "a putting to proof (by experiment [of good], experience [of evil], solicitation, discipline or provocation); by implication adversity :- temptation, × try. 3986 English Words used in KJV: temptation 19 temptations 1 try 1 [Total Count: 21] from <G3985> (peirazo). Strong's Dictionary.

15 Then, after desire has conceived, it gives birth to sin; and sin, when it is full-grown, gives birth to death.

God makes it clear through His earthly agent James that when we get dragged away and enticed by our own evil desires ("lust or passionate longing")[18], we will conceive them or in other words, "be captured, seized or taken"[19] by them! Then they will give birth to sin (sin is defined as "failure, missing the mark")[20] in us which will grow and eventually result in death! Simply put, if not dealt with properly and quickly, our evil desires can cause us to disobey God and miss His mark, resulting in sin, and our sin can bring dire consequences; even spiritual and physical death! These terrific results can also affect and even infect others around us. For a deeper discussion of this slippery slide into sin see Chapter 3 titled, "The FADE Into Sin."

Everyone faces temptation. No one is exempt. Even Jesus Christ, who was God in human form, was "tempted in every way, just as we are—yet was without sin." (Hebrews 4:15) Jesus set a great example for us, and He is able to sympathize with our weakness when we are tempted because of His experience. You might say,

---

[18] Evil Desires = ἐπιθυμία (epithumia) "desire, passionate longing, lust", 1939. NASB Dictionary. NASB and KJV use "lust." NIV, ESV, NLT and NKJV use "evil desires."

[19] Conceived = "Catch, Conceive, Seize, Take." συλλαμβάνω (syllambanō) Strong's Number: 4815, Part of Speech: v, Total Count: 16, from <G4862> (sun) and <G2983> (lambano); to clasp, i.e. seize (arrest, capture); specially to conceive (literal or figurative); by implication to aid :- catch, conceive, help, take. Strong's Talking Greek & Hebrew Dictionary.

[20] Sin = ἁμαρτία (hamartia) "a sin, failure", 266. Root: from 264 ἁμαρτάνω (hamartanō); "to miss the mark, do wrong." NASB Concordance and Thayers Greek Lexicon.

"Yeah, well, Jesus was God and I'm not, so what hope is there for me?" There is hope for you because the Bible says that God is at work in us who believe, as Philippians 1:6 states, "being confident of this, that He who began a good work in you will carry it on to completion until the day of Christ Jesus." Since God is in this relationship, it has to work—rather, it has to thrive! Especially if we will learn to FEAR God. The following acronym **FEAR** suggests 4 practical steps to take when staring temptation in the face:

Step 1. **F**ear and Love God,

Step 2. **E**scape from What Tempts You,

Step 3. **A**pply Scripture, and

Step 4. **R**emain Faithful to Christ.

Fear and Love God.

Why should we fear God? There are several reasons to hold a deep reverence and healthy respect[21] for an all powerful holy God, but note first that true knowledge[22] begins with fear that fools don't like or live by; "The fear of the Lord is the beginning of knowledge; Fools despise wisdom and instruction." (Proverbs 1:7, NASB)

---

[21] Fear = (also used as infinitive); moral reverence, dreadful, exceedingly, fear (-fulness). הָאְרֵי (yir'â Phonetic Pronunciation: yir-aw) 3374, Root: from H3373, in KJV: fear 41 exceedingly H1419, 2 dreadful 1 fearfulness 1 [Total Count: 45] Strong's Dictionary.

[22] Knowledge = cunning, know (-ledge), [un-] awares (wittingly), concern, premeditation, skill, truth. תַעַד (daath) 1847, from יָעַד (yada`) H3045 = a primitive root; to know (properly to ascertain by seeing); used in a great variety of senses, figurative, literal, euphemism and inference (including observation, care, recognition; and causative instruction, designation, punishment, etc.) Stong's Dictionary and NASB Concordance.

21

Reason number one to fear God, is because *He is Holy*, "Your ways, O God, are holy. What god is so great as our God?" (Psalms 77:13) Holiness is defined in this passage as something "consecrated, dedicated, clean, pure."[23] When the prophet Isaiah saw God's holiness, he responded in desperate shame and humility; "Woe to me.. I am ruined! For I am a man of unclean lips, and I live among a people of unclean lips, and my eyes have seen the King, the Lord Almighty." (Isaiah 6:5) Fortunately for him an angel brought a coal from the altar to cleanse him of his sin (v. 6)! And even better still for all of Christ's disciples; He died to pay the debt of sin once for all, "But now he has appeared once for all at the end of the ages to do away with sin by the sacrifice of himself." (Hebrews 9:26b)[24]

We should also revere God because *He Sees All.* As God spoke through the unknown writer of the letter to the Hebrews, "Nothing in all creation is hidden from God's sight. Everything is uncovered and laid bare before the eyes of him to whom we must give account." (Hebrews 4:13) In addition, the Psalms state, "From heaven the Lord looks down and sees all mankind" (Psalms 33:13) and Job declared, "His eyes are on the ways of men; he sees their every step." (Job 34:21) Just like a child who has discovered that his mom or dad is watching and starts to fearfully behave, we must be aware that a Holy God sees all that we do and should be more concerned with our own actions!

Lastly, we should fear God because *He is the Final Judge*, as Paul told the Corinthians "...He will bring to light what is hidden

---

[23] Holy = consecrated (thing), dedicated (thing), hallowed (thing), holiness, (× most) holy (× day, portion, thing), saint, sanctuary." קֹדֶשׁ (ko›-desh) 6944, from qādash = (verb) «to be (causat. make, pronounce or observe as) clean (ceremonial or moral) :- appoint, bid, consecrate, dedicate, defile, hallow, (be, keep) holy (-er, place), keep, prepare, proclaim, purify, sanctify.» Strong›s Dictionary.

[24] See also Hebrews 7:27; 9:12 and 1 Peter 3:18.

in darkness and will expose the motives of men's hearts..." (1 Corinthians 4:5b) The Bible further warns that everyone will be judged, "Just as man is destined to die once, and after that to face judgment." (Hebrews 9:27, see also Revelation 20:11-15) Surprisingly, Jesus even taught that every careless word was recorded, "But I tell you that men will have to give account on the day of judgment for every careless word they have spoken." (Matthew 12:36) Revelation informs us further that book records are kept, "And I saw the dead, great and small, standing before the throne, and books were opened. Another book was opened, which is the book of life. The dead were judged according to what they had done as recorded in the books." (Revelation 20:12)

Believers sometimes question whether or not they need to be concerned about God's judgment because of the His amazing and abundant grace. However, there is a time of judgment for believers too, for Paul told the church in Corinth, "For we must all appear before the judgment seat of Christ, that each one may receive what is due him for the things done while in the body, whether good or bad." (2 Corinthians 5:10) We can be better prepared for this coming event if we judge ourselves properly; "But if we judged ourselves, we would not come under judgment. When we are judged by the Lord, we are being disciplined so that we will not be condemned with the world." (1 Corinthians 11:31-32)

Thankfully, a lot of this judgment will include rewards, "For the Son of Man is going to come in his Father's glory with his angels, and then he will reward each person according to what he has done." (Matthew 16:27) Faith and trust in God adds greatly to it as well, "And without faith it is impossible to please God, because anyone who comes to him must believe that he exists and that he rewards those who earnestly seek him." (Hebrews 11:6)

Please read and be encouraged by this sampling of verses about God's rewards for faithful believers:

> Matthew 5:12 "Rejoice and be glad, because great is your reward in heaven, for in the same way they persecuted the prophets who were before you."

> Matthew 6:6 "But when you pray, go into your room, close the door and pray to your Father, who is unseen. Then your Father, who sees what is done in secret, will reward you."

> Matthew 10:41 "Anyone who receives a prophet because he is a prophet will receive a prophet's reward, and anyone who receives a righteous man because he is a righteous man will receive a righteous man's reward."

> Matthew 10:42 "And if anyone gives even a cup of cold water to one of these little ones because he is my disciple, I tell you the truth, he will certainly not lose his reward."

> Ephesians 6:8 "...because you know that the Lord will reward everyone for whatever good he does, whether he is slave or free."

> Colossians 3:24 "...since you know that you will receive an inheritance from the Lord as a reward. It is the Lord Christ you are serving."

> Hebrews 10:35 "So do not throw away your confidence; it will be richly rewarded."

> 2 John 1:8 "Watch out that you do not lose what you have worked for, but that you may be rewarded fully."

Escape from What Tempts You.

Before we check out God's escape plan from temptation, another ground rule must be established. God is not the tempter, "Let no one say when he is tempted, 'I am tempted by God'; for God cannot be tempted by evil, nor does He Himself tempt anyone." (James 1:13, NKJV) Since God is not the tempter and He is on our side—escape is possible, probable, doable!

The fact that escape is possible is stated clearly in 1 Corinthians 10:13 which promises, "No temptation has seized you except what is common to man. And God is faithful; He will not let you be tempted beyond what you can bear. But when you are tempted, He will also provide a way out so that you can stand up under it."

There are four important truths uncovered here about temptation. First, **temptation can "seize" us**, we can literally be caught or gripped[25] by it, hence the impending need for an escape.

Secondly, **temptation is not unique to anyone**. Note that this verse explains it "is common to man." Since it is common, the good news is that we should be able to get help from lots of people who have been in our shoes before.

Thirdly, **God will not allow us to be tempted beyond our breaking point**; "He will not let you be tempted beyond what you can bear." This is extremely encouraging news as God has promised we can break free from its grip!

---

[25] Seized = take, receive, catch, grip, get hold of. 2983, λαμβάνω, lambano, in KJV: receive 133, take 106, have 3, catch 3, not tr 1, miscellaneous translations 17 [Total Count: 263]. Strong's Dictionary.

25

Finally, **God will provide an escape route**[26] from the temptation; "He will also provide a way out..." Thank God there is a way out, we just need to look for it and take it! Second Timothy 2:22 adds an interesting formula for successful escape (I have added words in parentheses to show a consistent theme); "Flee (run from) the evil desires of youth, and pursue (run after) righteousness, faith, love and peace, along with (run with) those who call on the Lord out of a pure heart." Observe in this wise recommendation that our first action must be to *run from* temptation, to flee, escape or run away.[27]

Joseph, who is known for possessing "a coat of many colors" and who DreamWorks made an animated musical titled Joseph: King of Dreams, has the most amazing story of character and faithfulness to God detailed in Genesis 39:1-15, and provides a perfect example of escaping quickly from temptation. One day when the wife of the infamous Potiphar (captain of the Pharaoh's guard) happened to be in the house alone with Joseph, she tried (not for the first time) to get him to go to bed with her and she grabbed his coat as he wisely and quickly ran out of the house. He escaped![28] It is this type of prompt decision and action that is needed for us to find victory over temptation.

After we have run from temptation, we are then enabled to *run after* or pursue righteousness, a superior substitute for sinful

---

[26] A way out = an exit, outcome. 1545, ἔκβασις, ekbasis, Root: from 1544a; List of English Words and Number of Times Used: result (1), way of escape (1). NASB Concordance.

[27] Flee = to flee:—escape, run away. φεύγω (pheugô), 5343, Root: a prim. vb. Ibid.

[28] Genesis 39:11 "One day he went into the house to attend to his duties, and none of the household servants was inside. 12 She caught him by his cloak and said, "Come to bed with me!" But he left his cloak in her hand and ran out of the house.

thoughts. Professionals who help people break free from addictions and various other types of disorders, often refer to this as the replacement phase of Cognitive Behavioral Therapy (CBT).[29] The Bible stated a similar path to freedom 2000 years ago, "...take captive every thought to make it obedient to Christ." (2 Corinthians 10:5b) The positive thinking we need to employ is listed in Philippians 4:8; "Finally, brothers, whatever is true, whatever is noble, whatever is right, whatever is pure, whatever is lovely, whatever is admirable—if anything is excellent or praiseworthy—think about such things." Jesus also taught what our priorities should be, "Seek first the Kingdom of God and His righteousness and all these things will be added to you." (Matthew 6:33)

---

[29] CBT is an evidence-based form of psychotherapy that can be used to treat depression, mood disorders, anxiety disorders, severe mental illness, addiction, eating disorders, relational problems, and more. According to the American Psychological Association, "CBT is based on several core principles, including:
- Psychological problems are based, in part, on faulty or unhelpful ways of thinking.
- Psychological problems are based, in part, on learned patterns of unhelpful behavior.
- People suffering from psychological problems can learn better ways of coping with them, thereby relieving their symptoms and becoming more effective in their lives."

Unhelpful thinking patterns (or sometimes called cognitive distortions) can greatly affect one's mental, emotional, physical, spiritual, and relational health. Cognitive Behavioral Therapy helps people learn to find these unhelpful thinking patterns, evaluate them, and replace them with more helpful, truthful, life-giving thoughts.

This process can be how someone "takes every thought captive" and then "demolish arguments and every pretension that sets itself against the knowledge of God." It is a process that honors God because it can replace lies with truth, truths that lead people back to Him. https://seattlechristiancounseling.com/articles/how-does-thought-replacement-work-in-cognitive-behavioral-therapy. See also https://www.healthline.com/health/cognitive-restructuring.

The third ingredient found in this formula for victory, is finding someone to **run with**. Don't be afraid to ask someone who "calls on the Lord with a pure heart" to be an accountability partner with you. Someone who loves our heavenly Father and walks closely with Him through Bible reading, meditation, memorization, application and prayer. After all, athletes have coaches, musicians have instructors, and pastors have mentors.

Encouraging each other is extremely important to helping each other practice righteousness; "But encourage one another daily... so that none of you may be hardened by sin's deceitfulness." (Hebrews 3:13) Note that while the word "encourage" means "to comfort", it is mostly used in the New Testament to mean "to exhort, appeal... implore."[30] We must both comfort and implore each other to spiritual growth. Additionally, confession and prayer play an extremely important role in our healing and freedom in Christ, "Confess your sins to each other and pray for each other so that you may be healed." (James 5:16) This is often referred to as "accountability" or "brotherhood" and is extremely beneficial to one's growth and stability. Wisdom from the book of Proverbs adds, "As iron sharpens iron, so one man sharpens another."(Proverbs 27:17)

Flee in three, because eight is too late.

A great little poem to help us remember how quickly we should flee from temptation is, "Flee in three, because eight is too late." If we don't flee from what tempts us within three seconds, we will likely fail by the

---

[30] Encourage = to call to or for, to exhort, to encourage, comfort, appeal, beg, implore, plead, urge. παρακαλέω (parakaleô), 3870, from 3844 and 2564. NASB Concordance.

eighth second. A friend of mine suggested a similarly easy poem, "Flee in one, or you'll be done (as in 'done for')." The point is, a little sinful thinking can create a lot of spiritual stinking.

Apply Scripture.

James 1:22 challenges us with the importance of Bible application; "Do not merely listen to the word, and so deceive yourselves. Do what it says." The sooner we learn to apply Scripture the better! Not only do we have a command from our Lord for application, but we have a path forward where we can avoid deception in our lives. I can't imagine anyone wants to be deceived.

Remember a few paragraphs back we read Philippians 4:8 where we were advised to think righteously? Turning to 2 Timothy 3:16 we are taken deeper into this train of thought as it exhorts, "All Scripture is God-breathed and is useful for teaching, rebuking, correcting and training in righteousness." (see Chapter 18 for an in-depth explanation of this verse and the Biblical Education TEST). James adds, "Do not merely listen to the word, and so deceive yourselves. **Do what it says.** (James 1:22)

So how do we do this? How do we get the rubber to meet the road? Here are a few suggestions from Scripture:

Receive Jesus Christ as Lord and Savior of your life; this is the first and necessary step. Romans 10:9-10 reads, "That if you confess with your mouth, 'Jesus is Lord,' and believe in your heart that God raised him from the dead, you will be saved. For it is with your heart that you believe and are justified, and it is with your mouth that you confess and are saved." Moreover the Bible teaches that "...if anyone is in Christ, he is a new creation; the old has gone, the new has come!" (2 Corinthians 5:17)

Believe that the Holy Spirit guides you as 1 Corinthians 2:10-16 instructs;

> ...but God has revealed it to us by his Spirit. The Spirit searches all things, even the deep things of God. For who among men knows the thoughts of a man except the man's spirit within him? In the same way no one knows the thoughts of God except the Spirit of God. We have not received the spirit of the world but the Spirit who is from God, that we may understand what God has freely given us. This is what we speak, not in words taught us by human wisdom but in words taught by the Spirit, expressing spiritual truths in spiritual words. The man without the Spirit does not accept the things that come from the Spirit of God, for they are foolishness to him, and he cannot understand them, because they are spiritually discerned. The spiritual man makes judgments about all things, but he himself is not subject to any man's judgment: "For who has known the mind of the Lord that he may instruct him?" But we have the mind of Christ.

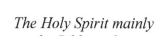

The Holy Spirit mainly uses the Bible to direct us.

Note that the Holy Spirit mainly uses the Bible to direct us, "...the sword of the Spirit... is the word of God." (Ephesians 6:17) The Bible is God's instruction book as we saw in 2 Timothy 3:16 and Hebrews 4:12, "For the word of God is living and active. Sharper than any double-edged sword, it penetrates even to dividing soul and spirit, joints and marrow; it judges the thoughts and attitudes of the heart." A couple useful acronyms for the **BIBLE** are this popular one: **Basic Instructions Before Leaving Earth**, and a new and possibly better one; Blessed Information to Begin Living Exceptionally.

Retrieve the word of God and change your thoughts to what God intended. Remember Philippians 4:8, a better and healthier way to think; "Finally, brothers, whatever is true, whatever is noble, whatever is right, whatever is pure, whatever is lovely, whatever is admirable—if anything is excellent or praiseworthy—think about such things." Paul also instructed the believers in the Grecian church in Corinth to "...take captive every thought to make it obedient to Christ" (2 Corinthians 10:5b) and Jesus Himself taught us the Great Commandment which includes loving God with our minds, "Love the Lord your God with all your heart and with all your soul and with all your mind and with all your strength.' The second is this: 'Love your neighbor as yourself.' There is no commandment greater than these." (Mark 12:30-31)

Achieve practical application of the Bible and become a user and doer of Scripture. It is through the practice of the teachings of God's inspired word that we are trained to discern what is right and wrong, as Hebrews 5:13-14 stresses, "Anyone who lives on milk, being still an infant, is not acquainted with the teaching about righteousness. But solid food is for the mature, who by constant use have trained themselves to distinguish good from evil." James 1:22-25 adds more;

> Do not merely listen to the word, and so deceive yourselves. Do what it says. Anyone who listens to the word but does not do what it says is like a man who looks at his face in a mirror and, after looking at himself, goes away and immediately forgets what he looks like. But the man who looks intently into the perfect law that gives freedom, and continues to do this, not forgetting what he has heard, but doing it—he will be blessed in

what he does.

Of great importance here is the example of the Lord Jesus Christ. Note in the following passage how He answers Satan's temptations every time with written Scripture:

> Then Jesus was led by the Spirit into the desert to be tempted by the devil. 2 After fasting forty days and forty nights, he was hungry.
>
> The tempter came to him and said, "If you are the Son of God, tell these stones to become bread."
>
> Jesus answered, "**It is written**: 'Man does not live on bread alone, but on every word that comes from the mouth of God.'"
>
> Then the devil took him to the holy city and had him stand on the highest point of the temple. 6 "If you are the Son of God," he said, "throw yourself down. For **it is written**:
>
> "'He will command his angels concerning you, and they will lift you up in their hands, so that you will not strike your foot against a stone.'"
>
> Jesus answered him, "It is also written: 'Do not put the Lord your God to the test.'"
>
> Again, the devil took him to a very high mountain and showed him all the kingdoms of the world and their splendor. 9 "All this I will give you," he said, "if you will bow down and worship me."
>
> Jesus said to him, "Away from me, Satan! For **it is written**: 'Worship the Lord your God, and serve him only.'"
>
> Then the devil left him, and angels came and attended him. (Matthew 4:1-10)

One final note on this passage: If Jesus responded to temptation with the word of God instead of direct rebuke, as He could have as God in human form, how much more should we as humans practice the memorization of God's word to be recited in our times of temptation!

Remain Faithful to Christ. Hebrews 3:14 informs us that it is extremely important to be faithful to Christ; "We have come to share in Christ if we hold firmly till the end the confidence we had at first." The word confidence here literally means to "stand by" Him,[31] so, as Jesus' disciples, we must stand by Him firmly to the end! When sharing the Parable of the Talents, Jesus said the owner commended the faithful servant and richly rewarded him for his faithfulness in procuring profitable investments, "Well done, good slave, because you have been faithful in a very little thing, you are to be in authority over ten cities." (Luke 19:17, NASB) Additionally, Hebrews 11:6 points to faith in God pleasing Him, "Without faith it is impossible to please God."

An important part of remaining faithful to God is our prayer life, as Romans 12:12 implores, "Be joyful in hope, patient in affliction, faithful in prayer." When teaching the disciples how to pray, Jesus said to pray about temptation also, "...And don't let us yield to temptation, but rescue us from the evil one." (Matthew 6:13, NLT) Keep praying and sharing your cares and concerns with God your Father, because He cares deeply for you! (1 Peter 5:7)

John Owen, an early American Puritan hit it dead on when he wrote about the dangerous effects of sin and how to address it, He wrote, "Be killing sin, or it will be killing you." Tough words

---

[31] Confidence = "a support, substance, steadiness", 5287 ὑπόστασις (hupostasis), Root: from 5259 (by, under) and 2476 (stand, e.g. stasis = "slowing or stopping"), literally "stand by (someone, something)." NASB Concordance.

for tough times—and especially relevant for today! One final word from Dr. Seuss who wisely reminds us that we make the choices that decide our future, "You have brains in your head. You have feet in your shoes. You can steer yourself any direction you choose."[32]

FEAR:

Fear and love God,
Escape from what tempts you,
Apply Scripture, and
Remain Faithful to Christ.

---

[32] Dr. Seuss. Oh the Places You'll Go! Random House, 1996, p.2.

Growing Deeper...

▶ Write out some Bible verses that you will recite next time you are tempted:

▶ Why not commit to memorizing these verses or have them close by for when temptation returns?

The Bible to Life

Chapter 5

You Are a VIP! Created in God's Image!

D id you know that God sees you as a VIP (very important person)? When God first made mankind, He created us in His own image! Genesis 1:26 says, "Then God said, 'Let Us make man in Our image, according to Our likeness...'" (NASB) That is pretty cool, isn't it? But what does it mean? What does it mean to be created in the "image of God?" The words "image" and "likeness" are defined similarly in Hebrew, except that the word "image" adds an extra dimension to the idea of being like God. It means that there is a respectability aspect or honor to mankind like that of God's. It certainly is not saying that we look like God physically, especially since God is spirit (John 4:24), but certainly our spirits are like His, possessing this splendorous respectability! God has made mankind to be much more like Him than anything else in all of creation! That should make us all feel better about who we are!

"Then the Lord God formed man of dust from the ground, and breathed into his nostrils the breath of life; and man became a living being (soul)." Genesis 2:7 (NASB)

Theologians talk about this honorable appearance unfolding in several different ways. They say that the image of God can be seen in men through imparted **transcendence**. In other words, just as God is above and greater than all of creation, so man is also above it. Of course, there still is a great difference between

God and man, as God does not need any of His creation. Man on the other hand, while transcending the natural world, absolutely needs it for his own physical survival. Further, man is designed to **rule** over creation according to Genesis 1:26-28. So, the first two of the amazing gifts of God to us in this gloriously shared image, are transcendence and rulership.

In addition, man is like God in his **personhood**. Man is a person just as God is a person. God is not human, but he is a person and He has personality. In that same vein, God is **sociable** and therefore so is man. Man is made to be a socially responsible human being and therefore has the awesome opportunity to experience a relationship with God! God said "let Us make man in Our image", which is believed to be a reference to the Holy Trinity—God the Father, God the Son and God the Holy Spirit. So just as God is three persons in one, man is made up of both body and spirit (and some add "soul"), and can even have oneness with a spouse. Remember, God said, "For this reason a man shall leave his father and his mother, and be joined to his wife; and they shall become one flesh." (NIV) Or as the NLT says, the two become "...united into one." (Genesis 2:24)

God also made mankind **creative** and procreative. Showing his creativity, Genesis 3:20 tells us Adam named his wife, and with meaning: "Now the man called his wife's name Eve, because she was the mother of all the living." Also, we read in Genesis 4:21 of Jubal (from where we get "jubilation") who was "...the father of all those who play the lyre and pipe." Music was one of the many creative traits of the image of God given to man. In reference to his procreative abilities, Genesis 4:1 states, "Now the man had relations with his wife Eve, and she conceived and gave birth to Cain, and she said, 'I have gotten a man child with the help of the Lord.'" Obviously, none of this could happen apart from God's power, yet in His sovereignty He gave man and woman the ability to conceive a child together as a result of their choice and action.

Another way in which God made us in His image was **productivity**. He designed mankind to work the garden of Eden and make it productive. According to Genesis 2:15, "The Lord God took the man and put him in the Garden of Eden to work it and take care of it." The NASB translates it "to cultivate it and keep it." Just as God worked, so man must work. And just as God rested after the sixth day, so man must rest after six days of work (Exodus 20:8-11).

The final manner in which we are created in God's image, is **goodness**. In Genesis 1:25, after creating everything but mankind, the text says that "God saw that it was good." After creating man, however, verse 31 notes that God then acknowledged that it was "very good." Also, a few verses later, chapter 2 verse 17 teaches that God gave Adam and Eve (humanity's parents and representatives) the potential to choose goodness with the tree of the knowledge of good and evil. They were good by God's design, but now they were afforded the opportunity to remain so, or by choice, fall from grace and possess knowledge of both good and evil. Subsequently, humanity became victims to their own flesh. Romans 5:18 states, "Consequently, just as the result of one trespass (Adam's) was condemnation for all men, so also the result of one act of righteousness was justification that brings life for all men." (NIV)

Being aware of who we are in Christ, is extremely important to our spiritual growth.

These seven characteristics of the image of God in which man was originally created have been

39

distorted due to sin. But when a person acknowledges God as Creator and Lord, and confesses their sin before Him, they have the opportunity to restore much of the image of God in themselves. In fact, 2 Corinthians 5:17 says that if we are in Christ, we are a new creation, and this verifies that we can be restored to our original image. Because of this transformation, we can be more like Christ and less like mankind. Being aware of who we are in Christ, is extremely important to our spiritual growth. This should encourage all of us who are believers to know that we are His special creation!

Romans 8:14 tells us that true Christians are the **sons of God** and are **led by His Spirit!** Verse 16 names us the **children of God** and according to verse 17 we are **heirs to God's kingdom!** Colossians 1:13-14 tells us that we are **forgiven,** Ephesians 2:8-9 says that we are **saved,** and Galatians 3:13 and Psalm 107:2 say that we have been **redeemed!** In other words, we have been bought with a price by God because He loves us so much and we are special to Him! First Corinthian's 5:7 says we've been **sanctified** (cleansed, made holy), Romans 5:1 says we are **justified,** and Colossians 1:13 says we have been **delivered!**

Psalm 91:11 says we are **safe,** Philippians 4:19 says we are **blessed,** and Deuteronomy 28:6 says we are **blessed continually!** First Peter 5:7 says we can be **carefree** and 1 Peter 2:24 says we are **healed!** First John 5:11-12 says we possess **eternal life,** Ephesians 6:10 and Philippians 4:13 say that we are **strong,** and Romans 8:37 says that we are **conquerors!** Revelation 12:11 and 1 John 4:4 say we are **over comers!** 1Cor. 4:17 says we've been **made faithful,** Romans 12:1-2 says we are **renewed in mind** and in Matthew 5:14 Jesus said we are "**the light of the world.**"

There is so much more the Bible says about who we are in Christ, but isn't this a great start? We should be encouraged by these verses and we will be wise to look at them from time to time as a reminder of His goodness and thank God for all He's done for us!

Growing Deeper...

▶ Set aside some time to commit some of these Bible verses to memory. If you think memorizing is difficult for you, start with just one verse and read it over 5 times a day for a week. You will have it memorized by the end of the week, guaranteed.

▶ Meditate on these 7 ways we have been made to be like God. How do they help you understand him better? Do you also understand yourself more?

The Bible to Life

Chapter 6

Exercising FAITH

Fully
And
Intentionally
Trusting
Him!

" **N** ow faith is the assurance of *things* hoped for, the conviction of things not seen." (Hebrews 11:1, NASB)

Jeb and Zeke were good friends and always looking for ways to turn a profit together. Jeb heard that the State of Montana was offering a bounty on wolves. They were paying $5000 a head to kill the wolves because they were becoming overpopulated and extremely dangerous. Jeb and Jeke headed to Montana and set up their tents out in the middle of the wilderness. The very next morning when Jeb woke up, he saw several hungry wolves outside the tent, and he frantically woke Zeke and warned him about it. When Zeke looked out and saw the wolves, he cried out confidently, "Jeb, we're rich!"

The word "faith" is defined as, "faith, faithfulness, proof"[33] and has the same root as "believes" in John 3:16, meaning, "to persuade, to have confidence, obey, trust." As we read through Hebrews 11,

---

[33] Faith = "faith, faithfulness, proof". πίστις (pistis), 4102, from root 3982; πείθω (peithô), meaning, "to persuade,

we certainly see how the tremendous acts of these Faith Hall of Famer's play out through their belief and obedience. Verse 4, for example states: "By faith Abel offered to God a better sacrifice than Cain..." (NASB) Note that you could substitute the word obedience for "faith." Then again in verse 7, "By faith (obedience) Noah, being warned *by God* about things not yet seen, in reverence prepared an ark for the salvation of his household..." (NASB) Abraham also in verse 8, was obedient, "By faith Abraham, when he was called, obeyed by going out to a place which he was to receive for an inheritance; and he went out, not knowing where he was going." (NASB)

To be clear, I am not trying to equate saving faith with obedience, for to do so would suggest that all who obeyed the Law were true believers, which is contrary to biblical teaching about God's grace in salvation.[34] Rather, I wish to show that true faith is expressed in obedience. Just as James writes:

> But someone will say, "You have faith; I have deeds." Show me your faith without deeds, and I will show you my faith by what I do.
>
> You believe that there is one God. Good! Even the demons believe that—and shudder.
>
> You foolish man, do you want evidence that faith without deeds is useless? Was not our ancestor Abraham considered righteous for what he did when he offered his son Isaac on the altar? You see that his faith and his actions were working together, and his faith was made

---

to have confidence, obey, trust." NASB Concordance.

[34] Ephesians 2:8-10 says, "For it is by grace you have been saved, through faith—and this not from yourselves, it is the gift of God—not by works, so that no one can boast. For we are God's workmanship, created in Christ Jesus to do good works, which God prepared in advance for us to do."

complete by what he did. (James 2:18-22)

It is most evident in the Scriptures that these men and women of God were **F**ully **A**nd **I**ntentionally **T**rusting **H**im by obeying His seemingly unrealistic requests. Such as when Noah built a ship on dry land, many miles from a large body of water, and Abraham, at 75 years of age, moved to a foreign land he had never seen, taking family and servants and herds of animals! This was real **FAITH**!

Three Levels of Belief

In our society today, there seem to be three levels of belief or faith in Jesus Christ that people may possess. The first level and largest group *believe about Jesus Christ*. A 2015 study revealed that 92% of Americans believed Christ was a real person,[35] however, only 56% believed He was God[36] and 52% believed He was sinless.[37] A shockingly tiny number of people today hold an entirely Biblical worldview of just 4%![38]

---

[35] "More than nine out of 10 adults say Jesus Christ was a real person who actually lived (92%). While the percentages dip slightly among younger generations—only 87 percent of Millennials agree Jesus actually lived—Americans are still very likely to believe the man, Jesus Christ, once walked the earth." https://www.barna.com/research/what-do-americans-believe-about-jesus-5-popular-beliefs/.

[36] "Most adults—not quite six in 10—believe Jesus was God (56%), while about one-quarter say he was only a religious or spiritual leader like Mohammed or the Buddha (26%). The remaining one in six say they aren't sure whether Jesus was divine (18%)." Ibid.

[37] "About half of Americans agree, either strongly or somewhat, that while he lived on earth, Jesus Christ was human and committed sins like other people (52%). Just less than half disagree, either strongly or somewhat, that Jesus committed sins while on earth (46%), and 2 percent aren't sure." Ibid.

[38] "According to Barna, as few as 6% of Americans held a biblical worldview in 2020 — half the number it was just 25 years prior. An additional

A true belief from a Biblical perspective requires a belief in Jesus Christ alone for salvation and eternal life: "For God so loved the world that he gave his one and only Son, that whoever believes in him shall not perish but have eternal life." (John 3:16) Jesus confirmed this view Himself and narrowed the meaning of faith down even more: "Jesus answered, 'I am the way and the truth and the life. No one comes to the Father except through me.'" (John 14:6) He also said, "Enter through the narrow gate. For wide is the gate and broad is the road that leads to destruction, and many enter through it. But small is the gate and narrow the road that leads to life, and only a few find it." (Matthew 7:13-14)

The second and deeper level of belief is to **believe in Jesus Christ**. According to 2 Corinthians 5:17, if one truly believes "in" Him they will be a "new creation": "Therefore, if anyone is in Christ, he is a new creation; the old has gone, the new has come!" According to the latest State of Theology Study compiled by Lifeway and sponsored by Ligonier Ministries, while most Americans agree that Jesus Christ is God's son (72%), they believe He is not God Himself (52%) and that He was created by God (55%).[39] So while most Americans believe about Jesus Christ, only half acknowledge His deity and believe in Him for salvation and eternal life.

---

national study conducted by Barna in 2023 revealed the number had fallen even further in the intervening two years with only 4% of Americans qualifying as having a biblical worldview." https://washingtonstand.com/commentary/worldview-refining-the-lens-through-which-we-see-everything-and-equipping-christians-to-change-the-world.

[39] "Half of Americans (52%) agree Jesus was a great teacher, but not God. Slightly more than half (55%) believe Jesus is the first and greatest being created by God, which runs contrary to the historical Christian belief that Jesus is eternal as God the Son." https://research.lifeway.com/2020/09/08/americans-hold-complex-conflicting-religious-beliefs-according-to-latest-state-of-theology-study/.

The third and deeper level of belief is to **believe Jesus Christ**. This level is for the disciple—the person who trusts in Jesus as God and His written word (the Bible) as truth. The Apostle John not only declared Jesus was "the way, the truth, and the life..." (John 14:6) but also as "the Word" Who "was God":

> In the beginning was the Word, and the Word was with God, and the Word was God. He was with God in the beginning.
>
> Through him all things were made; without him nothing was made that has been made. In him was life, and that life was the light of men.
>
> ...The Word became flesh and made his dwelling among us. We have seen his glory, the glory of the One and Only, who came from the Father, full of grace and truth. (John 1:1-4, 14)

Since Jesus is not here today in human form, the disciple of Jesus must now trust in His leading through the Holy Spirit and the Bible. A true disciple of Jesus must believe in the Bible as inerrant (without error), authoritative (having greatest authority in one's life) and infallible (meaning that it never fails to accomplish what God desires, like Isaiah 55:11 says[40]). If a person today does not believe in the Bible as God's inerrant

It is a weak and ailing faith that chooses a belief system on feelings and personal worldview alone.

---

[40] "...so is my word that goes out from my mouth: It will not return to me empty, but will accomplish what I desire and achieve the purpose for which I sent it." Isaiah (55:11)

and authoritative word, how can they believe in Jesus Christ for salvation and eternal life when it is the primary source for His existence and knowledge about Him and His plan for eternal life? It is a weak and ailing faith that chooses a belief system on feelings and personal worldview alone.

According to Gallup,

> A record-low 20% of Americans now say the Bible is the literal word of God, down from 24% the last time the question was asked in 2017, and half of what it was at its high points in 1980 and 1984. Meanwhile, a new high of 29% say the Bible is a collection of "fables, legends, history and moral precepts recorded by man." This marks the first time significantly more Americans have viewed the Bible as not divinely inspired than as the literal word of God. The largest percentage, 49%, choose the middle alternative (inspired word of God), roughly in line with where it has been in previous years."[41]

Having a saving and strong faith requires us to be fully and intentionally trusting Him!

Fully
And
Intentionally
Trusting
Him!

---

[41] https://news.gallup.com/poll/394262/fewer-bible-literal-word-god.aspx.

Growing Deeper...

▶ Which level of belief would you describe is yours?

▶ Do you hold to a Biblical worldview?

▶ Have you believed in Jesus Christ alone for your salvation and eternal life with Him?

The Bible to Life

Chapter 7

Fire Your RPG

Rejoice always,
Pray without ceasing, and
Give thanks in all circumstances.

" **R**ejoice always, pray continually, give thanks in all circumstances; for this is God's will for you in Christ Jesus." 1 Thessalonians 5:16-18

An RPG is a rocket propelled grenade that was developed to disarm army tanks. Upon impact, the RPG-7's grenade can penetrate up to 13 inches of metal and travel up to 900 meters in a few seconds to a target before it self-destructs. It can be carried easily since it only weighs 14.5 lbs. unloaded, and 19 lbs. loaded.[42] It is certainly a weapon to be feared in combat.

As disciples of Jesus Christ, we too have an **RPG** that can be fired endlessly at our spiritual enemy[43] resulting in major damages to his army and territory. It is the command of God found in 1 Thessalonians 5:16-18. Here, as part of the Lord's army,[44]

---

[42] https://www.military.com/daily-news/2019/06/07/how-rpg-works.html

[43] 1 Peter 5:8 "Be of sober *spirit,* be on the alert. Your adversary, the devil, prowls around like a roaring lion, seeking someone to devour." (NASB)

[44] Ephesians 6:10-17 states; "Finally, be strong in the Lord and in his mighty power. 11 Put on the full armor of God so that you can take your stand against the devil's schemes. 12 For our struggle is not against flesh and

our orders are to **R**ejoice always, **P**ray continuously and to **G**ive thanks in all circumstances. We know this command is powerful and effective because it "...is God's will" for us!

The word rejoice means "to be glad, fare well, be joyous."[45] Since we are commanded to be joyous and glad, it is obviously up to us to choose it. Many sociologists will tell us that we are a product only of our environment or our DNA, but here we are informed that we have a choice over our outlook and attitude! Who would you rather spend time with, people who are joyous or gloomy? Sad or happy? What type of person do you choose to be? If God commands us to rejoice, we are able to do it. Why not choose joy?

Prayer is also part of our marching orders. We will consider prayer later in more detail in chapter 10, so for now let's focus on how this passage says we are to converse with God. It instructs us to pray "without ceasing" which also means to speak with God our Father "incessantly, constantly, unceasingly... uninterruptedly."[46] Is that familiar to you? Do you spend

---

blood, but against the rulers, against the authorities, against the powers of this dark world and against the spiritual forces of evil in the heavenly realms. 13 Therefore put on the full armor of God, so that when the day of evil comes, you may be able to stand your ground, and after you have done everything, to stand. 14 Stand firm then, with the belt of truth buckled around your waist, with the breastplate of righteousness in place, 15 and with your feet fitted with the readiness that comes from the gospel of peace. 16 In addition to all this, take up the shield of faith, with which you can extinguish all the flaming arrows of the evil one. 17 Take the helmet of salvation and the sword of the Spirit, which is the word of God."

[45] Rejoice = "be glad, be joyous, fare well." χαίρω (chairô), 5463. NASB Concordance and Strong's Dictionary.

[46] Without ceasing = "incessantly, constantly, unceasingly." ἀδιαλείπτως (adialeiptôs) 89. Root: adv. from 88; (adialeiptos); "uninterruptedly, i.e. without omission (on an appropriate occasion) :- without ceasing." Ibid.

time with the Father constantly? Brother Lawrence[47] called this "practicing the presence of God", which means to be aware of His presence with us anywhere, anytime. He testified, "I have abandoned all particular forms of devotion, all prayer techniques. My only prayer practice is attwention. I carry on a habitual, silent, and secret conversation with God that fills me with overwhelming joy."[48]

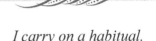

I carry on a habitual, silent, and secret conversation with God that fills me with overwhelming joy.

Our orders also include thankfulness in all circumstances. James, the leader of the Jerusalem church after Peter, wrote, "Consider it pure joy, my brothers, whenever you face trials of many kinds, because you know that the testing of your faith develops perseverance. Perseverance must finish its work so that you may be mature and complete, not lacking anything." (James 1:2-4) Trials should be a place for rejoicing because they will bring perseverance and eventually maturity in Christ!

Baseball legend Yogi Berra was taunting Hank Aaron at the plate during a regular season game, trying to distract him. He teased, "You know that the label on the bat should be facing up so you will hit better." Hank ignored him, took the next pitch that came over the plate and sent it streaking out over left field

---

[47] Brother Lawrence (1614–1691) was a French Carmelite monk of the 17th century. "Lawrence was a gentle and humble man who, despite his lack of education, just radiated holiness—not from the abbot's chair but from the kitchen where he worked." https://cac.org/daily-meditations/practicing-the-presence-of-god-2021-07-15/.

[48] Ibid.

into the bleachers for the home run. As he came back to home plate, he looked at Yogi and boasted, "I didn't come here to read."

As soldiers in Christ's army, we didn't come to read either! Let's shoot some RPG's!

RPG:

Rejoice always
Pray without ceasing
Give thanks in all circumstances

Growing Deeper...

▶ Are you a joyful person or do you find yourself complaining and being internally and/or outwardly grouchy?

▶ What do people say about you?

▶ Do you pray at various times during the day?

▶ Are you thankful for salvation? For God's mercy, grace and forgiveness? For food, shelter and a peaceful country?

The Bible to Life

Chapter 8

DENY Yourself

Do for others,
Enjoy God,
No to sin, and
Yield to God's will.

"Then Jesus said to His disciples, 'If anyone wishes to come after Me, he must **deny** himself, and take up his cross and follow Me.'" Matthew 16:24

If we are serious about being disciples of Jesus Christ, we must learn to **DENY** ourselves. To do so there are four simple, but not easy steps to follow:

Do to others.

First, a disciple must do to others as they would have others do for them. Jesus taught this "Golden Rule" in His famous Sermon on the Mount, "Therefore, whatever you want others to do for you, do also the same for them—this is the Law and the Prophets."

Putting the emphasis on others' needs helps us to better deny ourselves.

(Matthew 7:12) This important rule is later re-emphasized in the second half of the "Great Commandment" as "...love your neighbor as yourself." (Matthew 22:37, Mark 12:30) Putting the emphasis on others' needs helps us to better deny ourselves.

A recipient of several gold medals, Derek Redman ran for the British team in the 4 x 400 meter relay in the 1992 Olympic Games in Barcelona. Shortly after receiving the baton, he turned the corner and pulled his hamstring. Pictures and videos showed him laying on the track, defeated and broken. However, you could've heard a pin drop when he started limping towards the finish line. It was taking so long that an older man came down from the seats, and helped him walk the rest of the way. When they got across the finish line, the crowd stood up and gave Redman a standing ovation, even greater than they did for the race winners! He finished his race, because he let his father carry him! Although Redmond was disqualified and listed as not finishing due to outside assistance, the incident became a well-remembered moment in Olympic history, having been the subject of one of the International Olympic Committee's "Celebrate Humanity" videos. It was even used in advertisements by Visa as an illustration of the Olympic spirit and featured in Nike's "Courage" commercials in 2008.[49] Redman's dad certainly understood this principle.

Enjoy God.

Secondly, Jesus taught that we should enjoy God. We also see this in the first part of the Great Commandment where Jesus quoted the Shema (from Deuteronomy 6:4-5) and stated, "and you shall love the Lord your God with all your heart, and with all your soul, and with all your mind, and with all your strength." The Psalmist wrote a similar sentiment a thousand years earlier

---

[49] https://www.olympedia.org/athletes/69416. https://en.wikipedia.org/wiki/Derek_Redmond.

by scripting, "Delight yourself in the Lord; And He will give you the desires of your heart." (Psalms 37:4)

A high school football player who seemed to not take the game seriously always sat on the bench for games. One time in an important game, the first, second, and third strings all got injured or fouled out of the game, so the coach called on the fourth string which included the young joker. When he got out on the field, he surprisingly played like an all-state athlete! After the game, the coach was so pleased that he apologized to the young man for underestimating him and asked him what had changed. The young man joyfully answered, "my father was blind, and he passed away yesterday. So this is the first time he got to see me play!" The young football player loved his father and was ecstatic to get to play for him. We get to play this game of life everyday for our Heavenly Father, so enjoy God!

No to pleasures that lead to sin.

Thirdly, one must say no to pleasures that lead to sin. Paul wrote to Timothy, "Now flee from youthful lusts and pursue righteousness, faith, love *and* peace, with those who call on the Lord from a pure heart." (2 Timothy 2:22) When we learn to say no to sin, we cause our spiritual enemy great pains and defeat as James 4:7 informs, "Submit to God, resist the Devil and he will flee from you." Remember our discussion in Chapter 4 about Joseph and how he ran away from his temptation by Potiphar's wife? We need to build this same kind of intentional intensity to habitually say no to sin into our lives as well!

Yield to God's will.

Finally, it is absolutely necessary to yield to God's will. When teaching the disciples to pray, Jesus instructed them and us to commit to God's will in our prayers; "Your kingdom come. Your will be done, on earth as it is in heaven." (Matthew 6:10) For more on yielding to God's will in prayer, see Chapter 10 where this is discussed in more detail under the section titled "Yield to God's Will." For more on God's will in general, go to Chapter 19: SIR, the Three Wills of God, and to read about God's specific calling in your life, head to chapter 20: Everyone is CALLED.

DENY:

Do for others,
Enjoy God,
No to sin, and
Yield to God's will.

Growing Deeper...

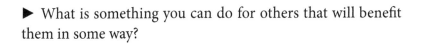

▶ What is something you can do for others that will benefit them in some way?

▶ How do you enjoy God privately and publicly?

▶ What sin do you need to start saying "no" to? How will you keep strong against it? (see Chapter 4 for more ideas)

▶ Are you doing God's will now? What do you need to change to do it?

The Bible to Life

Chapter 9

SERVE Christ

Share with others,
Endure the hardships of ministry,
Read the Bible,
Victorious over sin, and
Engage righteousness.

If you drop something in water you will see ripples on its surface making their way to the edges. I noticed this on a grand scale one time when flying in an airplane. I looked down at the massive lake far below us and there was one solitary speed boat cruising in the middle of the still waters. What caught my attention was the fact that the wake from the boat kept expanding until it hit the shoreline on each side. The only thing keeping the wake from growing even further were the solid banks on the sides of the lake.

The Apostle Paul reminds his "son" in the faith Timothy in Second Timothy chapter 2 to make ripples and wakes in his ministry. The acronym **SERVE** arises from a close examination of this challenge.

Share with others.

The first point Paul and the Holy Spirit make is that we must **Share** with others from what we have received from the Lord,

"You then, my son, be strong in the grace that is in Christ Jesus. And the things you have heard me say in the presence of many witnesses entrust to reliable men who will also be qualified to teach others." (2 Timothy 2:2)

There is a multiplication effect that occurs when we share what we have learned from Godly leaders and mentors with others.

There is a multiplication effect that occurs when we share what we have learned from Godly leaders and mentors with others, particularly if they are "reliable" or "faithful" as most translations put it.[50]

When I was a teenager, I met a youth pastor from a church of a different denomination from the one I had grown up in and his church was several miles further away from my home. I loved Pastor Doug and the youth group because he wanted to make disciples of Jesus and practiced this principle of sharing and multiplying. Needless to say, he and his wife had a profound effect on my life, and I and other youth group members have since gone on to help other new believers grow in their faith. The ripple effect was real and life changing!

Endure the hardships of ministry.

When I was training for basketball in middle school, high school and college, there were two things that were consistent between the different levels of training; endurance exercises and drills. We would run through them over and over so that we would accomplish the two goals of developing endurance and

---

[50] NASB, HCSB, NRSV, NKJV, KJV.

memory reflex. Endurance was absolutely necessary for playing 40 minute games at the top of our running speed. It paid great dividends to be in top shape. Often, the team in the best condition, was the team that achieved victory.

The next big idea coming out of this passage is the truth that we need to learn to **Endure** the difficulties of being a disciple of Jesus Christ. To "endure" is to "bear evil treatment, suffer hardship."[51]

Like the good soldier, the competing athlete and the hardworking farmer, we should desire to please God (our commanding officer), follow His commands (rules of the game) and share in the rewards (harvested crops) of ministry:

> **Endure** hardship with us like a good soldier of Christ Jesus. No one serving as a soldier gets involved in civilian affairs—he wants to please his commanding officer. Similarly, if anyone competes as an athlete, he does not receive the victor's crown unless he competes according to the rules. The hardworking farmer should be the first to receive a share of the crops. Reflect on what I am saying, for the Lord will give you insight into all this. Remember Jesus Christ, raised from the dead, descended from David. This is my gospel, for which I am suffering even to the point of being chained like a criminal. But God's word is not chained. Therefore I **endure** everything for the sake of the elect, that they too may obtain the salvation that is in Christ Jesus, with eternal glory.
> Here is a trustworthy saying: If we died with him, we

---

[51] Endure Hardship = "to bear evil treatment along with, endure hardship, suffer hardship, suffering." συγκακοπαθέω, (sugkakopatheô), 4777. NASB Concordance.

will also live with him; if we **endure**, we will also reign with him. If we disown him, he will also disown us; if we are faithless, he will remain faithful, for he cannot disown himself. Keep reminding them of these things. Warn them before God against quarreling about words; it is of no value, and only ruins those who listen. (2 Timothy 2:3-14)

Read the Bible.

"Do your best to present yourself to God as one approved, a workman who does not need to be ashamed and who correctly handles the word of truth." (2 Timothy 2:15)

The best way to serve someone is to listen to what they have asked to be done. Similarly, the best way to serve Christ is to know what He wants us to do. The most conclusive way to do this is to Read and Research His inerrant, infallible and authoritative word[52], His BIBLE, or "Basic Instructions Before Leaving Earth." As the last verse states, we should be like a "...workman who does not need to be ashamed..." because he "correctly handles the word of truth."

Victorious over sin.

For many years I led a Bible study with a ministry to alcoholics and drug addicts, and to my surprise, they were normal people who just happened to get addicted! The main difference

---

[52] Inerrant = "Without error." Infallible = "Does not fail to accomplish what God intends" (see also Isaiah 55:11). Authoritative = "Having full authority over one's life." The doctrine of the authority and inerrancy of Scripture is that, as a corollary of the inspiration of Scripture, the God-breathed Scriptures are wholly true in all things that they assert in the original autographs and therefore function with the authority of God's own words." The Gospel Coalition, https://www.thegospelcoalition.org/essay/authority-inerrancy-scripture/.

between them and other "normal" people was that their sin was obvious to others at some point due to the chemical takeover of their bodies and wills. Because this program was a Bible-based program, most of the addicts found freedom in Christ from their addictions!

The fact is, we all need victory over sin, and many sins are addictive once we have yielded to them. The key to victory over sin is to ACT on it; Acknowledge and Confess it, and Turn away from it, never going back to it (see chapter 2, ACT on Your Sin).

Please take note of verse 19 below where it says, "Everyone who confesses the name of the Lord must turn away from wickedness." We are here given the command to "turn away" from our sin of our own will if we are a confessor of Christ. Note also that we are held responsible for turning either way we decide. Verse 21 builds on this notion when it states that each one must cleanse him/herself! Victory comes from self-discipline and brings with it nobility, holiness and usefulness to God!

> Avoid godless chatter, because those who indulge in it will become more and more ungodly. Their teaching will spread like gangrene. Among them are Hymenaeus and Philetus, who have wandered away from the truth. They say that the resurrection has already taken place, and they destroy the faith of some.
> Nevertheless, God's solid foundation stands firm, sealed with this inscription: "The Lord knows those who are his," and, "Everyone who confesses the name of the Lord must **turn away from wickedness.**"
> In a large house there are articles not only of gold and silver, but also of wood and clay; some are for noble purposes and some for ignoble. If a man **cleanses himself** from the latter, he will be **an instrument for noble**

purposes, made holy, useful to the Master and prepared to do any good work. (2 Timothy 2:16-21)

Are you Victorious over sin and being used by the Master?

Engage righteousness.

Our Heavenly Father so wants us to Engage or "pursue" righteousness! In verse 22, if we replace the words "Flee" and "pursue" with the words "run from" and "run after" and then add "run" one more time, it may help illuminate the meaning more. "**Run from** the evil desires of youth, and **run after** righteousness, faith, love and peace, **run** along with those who call on the Lord out of a pure heart." (as discussed in Chapter 4, section 2) Pursuing someone or something takes effort. How about getting some spiritual exercise by running after and Engaging righteousness?

In the final section of chapter 2, the words that make up this acronym **SERVE** have been added in parentheses to point to its relevance:

Flee the evil desires of youth (**Victorious**), and pursue (**Engage**) righteousness, faith, love and peace, along with those who call on the Lord out of a pure heart. Don't have anything to do with foolish and stupid arguments, because you know they produce quarrels. And the Lord's servant must not quarrel; instead, he must be kind to everyone, able to teach (**Share**), not resentful. Those who oppose him (**Endure**) he must gently instruct, (**Share**) in the hope that God will grant them repentance (**Victorious**) leading them to a knowledge of the truth (**Read** the Word), and that they will come to their senses and escape from the trap of the devil (**Victorious**), who has taken them captive to do his will.

SERVE:

Share with others,
Endure the hardships of ministry,
Read/**R**esearch the Bible,
Victorious over sin, and
Engage righteousness

Growing Deeper...

▶ Are you sharing the truths of the Gospel and the Word of God with others? Do you have someone who you are discipling for Jesus to become like Him?

▶ How is your endurance? Are you being treated poorly because of your faith? What are you doing to get stronger?

▶ Download a Bible app like Blue Letter Bible and type in "endurance" and meditate on the verses it recommends.

▶ How is your battle with sin? Are you gaining or losing ground in the struggle?

▶ It may be helpful to think of the difficulty with sin like climbing a staircase. Although you may slip back down the stairs a step or two, remember that you have taken several steps upward and you can be encouraged to step up again now that you have ACTed!

▶ How are you Engaging righteousness? Is there more you can do? Is there something you should change?

The Bible to Life

Chapter 10

Say Your PRAYERS

Praise God,
Requests,
Admit sin,
Yield to God's will,
Enlist in His work,
Resist temptation, and
Stand against Satan.

A preacher and a New York City taxi driver both died the same day and went to heaven. They saw Saint Peter at the gate and told him who they were. The taxi driver explained, "I was a New York City taxi driver." To which Peter replied, "I know who you are and that mansion up on the hill is yours."

After hearing that conversation, the pastor thought to himself "I've really got this in the bag, there must be something extra special for me!" Peter said to the pastor, "And your heavenly home is that little shack at the bottom of the hill." The pastor was shocked and said, "I was a pastor, I preached the gospel and taught the word of God, and all I get is a shack!" Peter replied, "When you preached people fell asleep. When the New York City taxi driver drove, people prayed!"

Hopefully fast drivers aren't the only reason people pray, but certainly stressful events get our attention and have a way of getting our priorities realigned. Prayer is not complicated. The key to meaningful and answered prayers is relationship. If we keep in mind that God loves us and wants to spend time with us, then we can realize how important talking to Him is. If you love someone, you want to spend time with them and ask questions and share your inner feelings. Make your prayer time about loving God and you will find yourself in a growing relationship with Him. James

The key to meaningful and answered prayers is relationship.

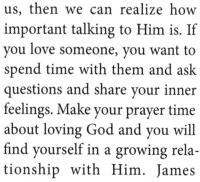

encouraged us to know that God will come near to us if we take some initiative in the relationship, "Come near to God and He will come near to you." (James 4:8) I don't know about you, but I get excited about that promise! Also, if you want to hear God speak, then reading the Bible is the key, as it is actually God's written words to us! Any healthy relationship includes both talking and listening.

In one of His speeches, Jesus told the crowd that God wants to give good gifts to His children.[53] Every believer is part of God's family and Jesus wants us to know it and come to God as our eternal, loving and faithful Father.[54] Just previously in

---

[53] Matthew 7:11, "If you, then, though you are evil, know how to give good gifts to your children, how much more will your Father in heaven give good gifts to those who ask him!" The Sermon on the Mount, Matthew chapters 5-7.

[54] "Father of Christians, as those who through Christ have been exalted to a specially close and intimate relationship with God, and who no longer dread him as the stern judge of sinners, but revere him as their reconciled and loving Father. This conception, common in the N.T. Epistles, shines forth with especial brightness in Romans 8:15; Galatians 4:6; in John's use of the term it seems to include the additional idea of one who by the power

the sermon, He offered a model for prayer which started with the words "Our Father in heaven..."[55] revealing God's parental longing for relationship with us, including provision and protection for His children. Take time to read Matthew chapters 5 through 7. It will be life-changing! Here are some excerpts:

> And when you pray, do not be like the hypocrites, for they love to pray standing in the synagogues and on the street corners to be seen by men. I tell you the truth, they have received their reward in full. But when you pray, go into your room, close the door and pray to your **Father**, who is unseen. Then your **Father**, who sees what is done in secret, will **reward** you. And when you pray, do not keep on babbling like pagans, for they think they will be heard because of their many words. Do not be like them, for your **Father** knows what you need before you ask him.
> This, then, is how you should pray: "Our **Father** in heaven, hallowed be your name, your kingdom come, your will be done on earth as it is in heaven.
> Give us today our daily bread.
> Forgive us our debts, as we also have forgiven our debtors.
> And lead us not into temptation, but deliver us from the evil one." (Matthew 6:5-13)
>
> Ask and it will be given to you; seek and you will find; knock and the door will be opened to you. For everyone who asks receives; he who seeks finds; and to him who knocks, the door will be opened.
> Which of you, if his son asks for bread, will give him

---

of his Spirit, operative in the gospel, has begotten them anew to a life of holiness." *Pater*, #3962, Greek-English Lexicon of the New Testament.

[55] Matthew 6:9.

a stone? Or if he asks for a fish, will give him a snake? If you, then, though you are evil, know how to give good gifts to your children, how much more will your **Father in heaven give good gifts to those who ask him!** (Matthew 7:7-11)

A few things bear explanation in these passages on prayer. First, the word "hypocrite" in 6:5 means "actor"[56]. Not unlike television and movie actors today, these religious leaders were not who they wanted people to think they were, and enjoyed their applause and popularity. The problem was, Jesus said, that they got only praise from men, and there could be so much more for them than that. Believers who pray in secret asking God for their provision will be rewarded by God Himself (6:6) and He has so much to give, in fact everything is His![57] I don't know about you, but I would rather receive good gifts from my generous loving Father God that are immeasurable and many of which are eternal, rather than temporary praise from men, who in the next breath may curse, slander or even persecute me.

In verse 7, Jesus warned about the "babbling" of the hypocrites because they were wrong to think they would be heard because of their many words. In fact, this word means "stammering"[58], suggesting that they don't even know how to pray or what to pray about, so Jesus teaches them what is traditionally called

---

[56] Hypocrite = *Hupokrites*, # 5723. NASB Concordance.

[57] "For every animal of the forest is mine, and the cattle on a thousand hills. I know every bird in the mountains, and the creatures of the field are mine." Psalms 50:10-11. "Every good and perfect gift is from above, coming down from the Father of the heavenly lights, who does not change like shifting shadows." James 1:17.

[58] Babbling = *battalogeô*, #945. NASB Concordance.

"The Lord's Prayer". Maybe the following acronym "**PRAYERS**" will help you understand and remember it:

Praise God

After addressing God as Father, Jesus encourages us to praise Him by revering His holiness; "hallowed be thy name…" God alone is holy or blameless and pure[59] and praise belongs to Him alone! "Praise be to the Lord God… who alone does marvelous deeds." (Psalms 72:18) It is quite significant that Jesus wanted us to start our prayers with praise as it is the opposite of what we naturally do. We tend to jump into prayer asking God for personal requests, like more money, better health, etc. James warned that we won't get what we ask for when we ask with the wrong motives and want to spend it on our own pleasures (James 4:3).

Requests

Most common among the parts of prayer has got to be requests, asking God for things; "give us today our daily bread…" This has to do with needs, not wants.[60] God has promised to provide for food and shelter, and everything else He gives us is a bonus! Since He wants to give us "good gifts" as we see in 7:11, He may choose to do much more for us than "daily bread" if we ask!

When I read the small but potent book titled "The Prayer of Jabez" by Bruce Wilkinson, I was intrigued with Jabez's request and God's affirmative response to it. Jabez asked to be free from pain and have his territory expanded (more land assets and wealth):

---

[59] Holy = *hagiazō*, #37, #40. Strong's Concordance.

[60] See Matthew 6:28-33.

> Jabez was more honorable than his brothers. His mother had named him Jabez, saying, 'I gave birth to him in pain.' 10 Jabez cried out to the God of Israel, 'Oh, that you would bless me and enlarge my territory! Let your hand be with me, and keep me from harm so that I will be free from pain.' And God granted his request. (1 Chronicles 4:9-10)

It is notable that Jabez was "honorable" and sounds like the kind of believer Jesus referenced who would hear one day from God, "Well done good and faithful servant." (Matthew 25:23) Psalms 84:11b promises, "...No good thing does He (God) withhold from those who walk uprightly" and "God, who richly provides us with everything for our enjoyment." (1 Timothy 6:17b). Note the fact that God answered Jabz's seemingly selfish prayer![61] What a great Father we have in heaven, full of love for His cherished children!

Admit Sin

When my son Matt was a three-year old, he didn't like vegetables much. So when I told him one time "clean your plate", which meant to eat everything on it, he grabbed his napkin and meticulously began to push off the veggies and wipe the plate clean. Then when he was finished, he looked at me with a satisfied and proud expression on his face, and hilariously exclaimed, "Look daddy, I cleaned my plate!"

As born-again believers we have had our plates cleaned—we have been forgiven of all our sins![62] However, as believers we still have

---

[61] James 4:3 balances what we ask for, with our motivation in asking, "When you ask, you do not receive, because you ask with wrong motives, that you may spend what you get on your pleasures."

[62] "But now that you have been set free from sin and have become slaves to God, the benefit you reap leads to holiness, and the result is eternal

the ability to disobey God, and when we do we need to admit or confess our acts to God right away. That is why Jesus said to pray "forgive us for our debts[63]..." and in the parallel passage in Luke 11:4, the word "sin" is used in place of "debts". So "debts" must be used by Matthew to mean moral debts. The word for "sin" in the Luke passage means "a sin, failure, offense", from a root word meaning "to miss the mark, do wrong."[64] In other words, we should be regularly asking God to forgive us for our sins, those times when we failed to hit the mark He set for us. First John 1:9 promises that He will pardon us, "If we confess our sins, He is faithful and just and will forgive us our sins and purify us from all unrighteousness."

In addition, 1 John 2:28 warns us to walk always with Christ and be ready for His return; "Now, little children, abide in Him, so that when He appears, we may have confidence and not shrink away from Him in shame at His coming." (NASB) Second Corinthians 5:10 observes, "For we must all appear before the judgment seat of Christ, that each one may receive what is due him for the things done while in the body, whether good or bad." Since there are actions believers can take that are bad and sinful, admitting our sin to God daily is of the utmost importance to staying clean. If we abide or remain in Christ, we will not have to deal with shame and regret when we stand before Him at His return.

Yield to God's will

I am amazed that this verse doesn't say "show us your will", which is usually a top question among Christians. Instead it reads, "Your

---

life." Romans 6:22

[63] Debts meaning "That which is owed, a debt." = *opheilēma*, #3783. NASB Concordance.

[64] Sin = harmatia, #266. Ibid.

will be done." We are not told in Scripture to pray for details of God's will to be revealed to us, but rather to surrender to His will, whatever it may be. Not a very popular concept in today's culture.

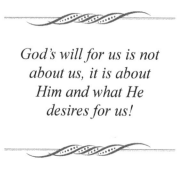

God's will for us is not about us, it is about Him and what He desires for us!

Keep in mind as well, that God's will for us is not about us—it is about Him and what He desires for us! Our prayer might look like this: "God show me your will for **ME**!" When it really ought to look like this: "God, show me **YOUR** will for me." God knows all and therefore knows best. He even knows what lies ahead![65]

When we yield and surrender to God's will, we can rest in the confidence that we will be taken care of in the best way possible.

The rest of the statement is, "just as it is in heaven." God's will is perfectly executed among the heavenly hosts, so our Lord wants us to ask for the same kind of result in our daily lives.

Enlist in His work

God is at work in the world establishing His Kingdom, which we who are believers are a part of. So when Jesus said to pray "Your Kingdom come..." it was connected with "Your will be done". After

---

[65] Jeremiah 29:11 "'For I know the plans I have for you,' declares the Lord, 'plans to prosper you and not to harm you, plans to give you hope and a future.'"

salvation[66] and righteousness[67], God's will is for us to help build His kingdom, but His kingdom is not about bricks and mortar, it is about souls! We are not to build streets, we are to walk the streets— telling others of Jesus and His work on the cross for us and everyone! Jesus Christ com- manded His disciples to "go and make disciples of all nations."

We are not to build streets, we are to walk the streets—telling others of Jesus and His work on the cross for us...

(Matthew 28:19-20) He also encouraged us to "seek first His (God's) kingdom and His righteousness..." (Matthew 6:33) It is a kingdom that exists in the future in heaven with God[68] and the present in the living universal Church (body) where He is the head.[69]

---

[66] 2 Peter 3:9 "The Lord is not slow in keeping his promise, as some under- stand slowness. He is patient with you, not wanting anyone to perish, but everyone to come to repentance."

[67] Matthew 6:33 "But seek first his kingdom and his righteousness, and all these things will be given to you as well." 1 Thessalonians 4:3 "It is God's will that you should be sanctified..." 1 Peter 2:15 "For it is God's will that by doing good you should silence the ignorant talk of foolish men."

[68] Revelation 21:1-4 "Then I saw a new heaven and a new earth, for the first heaven and the first earth had passed away, and there was no longer any sea. I saw the Holy City, the new Jerusalem, coming down out of heaven from God, prepared as a bride beautifully dressed for her husband. And I heard a loud voice from the throne saying, 'Now the dwelling of God is with men, and he will live with them. They will be his people, and God himself will be with them and be their God. He will wipe every tear from their eyes. There will be no more death or mourning or crying or pain, for the old order of things has passed away.'"

[69] Ephesians 4:15-16 "Instead, speaking the truth in love, we will in all things grow up into him who is the Head, that is, Christ. 16 From him the whole body, joined and held together by every supporting ligament, grows and builds itself up in love, as each part does its work."

Some of the tools God has given us to do this work are spiritual gifts, or gifts given by the Holy Spirit. Romans chapter 12 and 1 Corinthians chapters 12 through 14 offer lists of spiritual gifts which the Holy Spirit gives to all believers as He wishes (1 Corinthians 12:11) so we can better work as a body to do the work God wants us to do.

In addition, He has given us armor and weapons for the spiritual battle which Satan brings against believers to attempt our destruction. These weapons are truth, righteousness, the gospel, faith, assurance of salvation, the Bible, and prayer. This is a battle we can't see with our eyes, but is very real just the same, and it is one the devil cannot win when we remain in a close walk with Christ; "Submit yourselves, then, to God. Resist the devil, and he will flee from you." (James 4:7

Resist Satan

Jesus told us to pray about resisting Satan when he said "and lead us not into temptation…" This phrasing is a bit misleading for our modern vocabulary because it implies that the one being spoken to (God) can or will be responsible for our sin when we give in to temptation. Perhaps a better wording would be "do not allow us to be led into temptation." The reason for this sentence re-structuring is discovered when comparing this passage with James 1:13-14 which tells us that God does not tempt anyone, "When tempted, no one should say, 'God is tempting me.' For God cannot be tempted by evil, nor does He tempt anyone; but each one is tempted when, by his own evil desire, he is dragged away and enticed." The New Living Translation has phrased it this way; "And don't let us yield to temptation."

Stand against Satan

A few Bible translations end the prayer with a request to be delivered from evil, but most have translated it as "deliver us from the evil one." There are several reasons for this difference. First there is the article "the" in front of the word "evil" in Greek, so it should at least be written as "the evil" in modern English.[70] Secondly, evil does not exist apart from a person or being that rebels against God. And thirdly, in our culture, we don't tend to think spiritually too often and therefore do not fully understand this statement, unless it is it personified for example, as "the Evil One". Finally, comparable Scriptures confirm that Satan and demons are what we need protection from, "For our struggle is not against flesh and blood, but against the rulers, against the authorities, against the powers of this dark world and against the spiritual forces of evil in the heavenly realms." (Ephesians 6:12)

One more thing, the word "deliver" means "to rescue, literally to draw to oneself, to set free."[71] We need to implore God to rescue us from Satan's schemes and attacks, by drawing us to Himself! Then the threat of Satan himself is nothing to be afraid of. A believer who walks daily with Christ, through prayer and resistance will only ever see our enemy's back as he turns tail and runs away! "Submit yourselves, then, to God. Resist the devil, and he will flee from you." (James 4:7)

A believer who walks daily with Christ, through prayer and resistance will only ever see our enemy's back as he turns tail and runs away... If you want to stand—kneel! The key to standing against Satan in battle, is to be kneeling before God in prayer!

---

[70] "The evil" = *tou ponerou*, # 4190. NASB Concordence.

[71] Deliver = *rhuomai*, #4506. Ibid.

If you want to stand—kneel! The key to standing against Satan in battle, is to be kneeling before God in prayer!

What do you think? Do you think you can go wrong following this method for PRAYERS that Jesus gave us?

If you don't care for acronyms, don't let that keep you from using this model prayer each day in your daily walk with the Lord! You can read it every time you pray or memorize it, then pray it with sincerity and passion (Jesus Himself prayed with loud cries and tears[72])! I like to use it as an outline, adding my own details as I pray, like "your will be done in my life as it is in heaven" and "protect me and my family from the evil one." Don't be afraid to make it your own by getting personal with God about the details. Talk to Him like you do anyone else you care about—just because you can't see Him, doesn't mean He is not there. Think of your cell phone calls (without video chat). You can't see the person on the other end of the line, but you know they are there anyway. Remember, God is waiting for you to talk with Him and spend time with Him!

PRAYERS:

Praise God,
Requests,
Admit sin,
Yield to God's will,
Enlist in His work,
Resist temptation, and
Stand against Satan.

---

[72] Hebrews 5:7 "During the days of Jesus' life on earth, he offered up prayers and petitions with loud cries and tears to the one who could save him from death, and he was heard because of his reverent submission."

Growing Deeper...

▶ Try keeping your own prayer journal. I have been writing in one for many years and it has been extremely encouraging and uplifting to me to look back and see what God has done in response to my prayers! In it I record all the people God has brought into my path who need either salvation, spiritual growth, encouragement, the Holy Spirit's guidance and power, physical, emotional, mental and spiritual healing, more resources, finances, etc. Along with all that, there are pages and pages of answers to those requests! Most of them positive! Sometimes God has clearly said "no", but most of the time He has said "yes"! Another thing I have learned, is that He often answers in different, yet better ways than I expected! And He has answered in His time frame, not mine! This is where faith[73] and waiting[74] on God come into play!

If you are like me, you may not want to write out long detailed requests and answers, and you don't have to. I always write mine down in point form so it looks more like a ledger than a journal, but it still is a very encouraging report for me to see what God has done for me and those for whom I pray! You can also dictate your list to an electronic device if you don't like handwriting or typing. I dictate lists to my phone and save them in the notepad, then I email it to my computer to print out on paper and put in my journal (which is in a binder). The important thing here is to keep a record of what God is doing with your prayers! It will be revolutionary to your prayer experience! Give it a try! You will be happy you did.

---

[73] Hebrews 11:6 "And without faith it is impossible to please God, because anyone who comes to him must believe that he exists and that he rewards those who earnestly seek him."

[74] Isaiah 40:31 "Yet those who wait for the Lord Will gain new strength; They will mount up *with* wings like eagles, They will run and not get tired, They will walk and not become weary." (NASB)

The Bible to Life

Chapter 11

HIT the Mark

Humble yourself,
Implore Jesus, and
Trust Him.

In the Gospel of Mark we read of a synagogue leader named Jairus who incidentally **HIT** the Mark as a father through his intercession with Jesus on his daughter's behalf. This happened because he **H**umbled himself before Jesus, **I**mplored Jesus to heal his daughter, and **T**rusted Jesus with her life.

Here is the account as recorded in Mark's Gospel, chapter 5:

> When Jesus had again crossed over by boat to the other side of the lake, a large crowd gathered around him while he was by the lake. Then one of the synagogue rulers, named Jairus, came there. Seeing Jesus, he fell at his feet and pleaded earnestly with him, "My little daughter is dying. Please come and put your hands on her so that she will be healed and live." So Jesus went with him...
>
> While Jesus was still speaking, some men came from the house of Jairus, the synagogue ruler. "Your daughter is dead," they said. "Why bother the teacher any more?"

Ignoring what they said, Jesus told the synagogue ruler, "Don't be afraid; just believe."

He did not let anyone follow him except Peter, James and John the brother of James. When they came to the home of the synagogue ruler, Jesus saw a commotion, with people crying and wailing loudly. He went in and said to them, "Why all this commotion and wailing? The child is not dead but asleep." But they laughed at him.

After he put them all out, he took the child's father and mother and the disciples who were with him, and went in where the child was. He took her by the hand and said to her, *"Talitha koum!"* (which means, "Little girl, I say to you, get up!"). Immediately the girl stood up and walked around (she was twelve years old). At this they were completely astonished. He gave strict orders not to let anyone know about this, and told them to give her something to eat. (Mark 5:21-24; 35-42)

Humble Yourself.

Note that verse 22 points out Jairus' humility as he fell at Jesus' feet. He willingly humbled himself by simply going to meet Jesus in the first place, someone who most Jewish leaders thought was just a controversial new rabbi, who was even deceiving people. Since Jairus had to have been well respected among the Jewish community in order to become the synagogue leader, he could easily have succumbed to arrogance about his position. The text is abundantly clear that Jairus was willing to follow Jesus' instructions in order to save his daughter.

Humility in the Bible is an important theme and means, "to make low, abase."[75] First Peter 5:5-6 directs this kind of lowliness;

> Young men, in the same way be submissive to those who are older. All of you, clothe yourselves with humility toward one another, because, "God opposes the proud but gives grace to the humble." Humble yourselves, therefore, under God's mighty hand, that He may lift you up in due time.

Also, James 4:10 adds, "Humble yourselves before the Lord, and He will lift you up."

Implore Jesus.

Next, we see in verse 23, that Jairus Implored Jesus to save his daughter. He "pleaded earnestly" with Jesus and said, "Please come and put your hands on her so that she will be healed and live." He was desperate. Sometimes desperation emboldens us to plead with someone so we get what we want.

When God informed Abraham that He was going to destroy Sodom and Gomorrah (Genesis 18:16-33), Abraham pleaded and negotiated with Him to spare the righteous who were there and was probably thinking of his nephew Lot and his family. He questioned God and asked if He would spare the cities if there were 50 righteous people, then 40, 30, 20 and even 10! God replied to Abraham that He would if He found 10 righteous souls. Sadly, He did not find even that small amount! However,He did send angels into the cities to rescue Lot and his wife and daughters

---

75 Humble = "to make low, to make humble, abase." ταπεινόω, (tapeinoô), 5013. Root: from 5011; (tapeinos) = "to depress; figurative to humiliate (in condition or heart)." NASB Dictionary & Strong's Dictionary.

(Genesis 19:1-29). Abraham implored God to intervene and Lot and his family were saved (except for his wife who disobeyed and looked back)!

God encourages us through the Apostle Paul to not be afraid to petition Him. In Philippians 4 he writes, "Do not be anxious about anything, but in everything, by prayer and petition, with thanksgiving, present your requests to God. And the peace of God, which transcends all understanding, will guard your hearts and your minds in Christ Jesus." (Philippians 4:6-7) Note the word "petition" means, "a need, entreaty, prayer" and comes from two root words meaning, "ask, beg, implore" and further back to mean, "to tie, bind."[76] God expects us to beg Him or tie Him to helping others in need.

Trust Him.

Finally, we find Jairus putting unwavering Trust in Jesus. So much so, that when he was told of his daughter's passing (verse 35), he completely ignored the reporters and followed Jesus back to his house. There he got to witness his precious daughter's miraculous resurrection at the hands of his Creator![77] What joy he must have experienced to see her health completely

---

[76] Petition = "a need, entreaty, prayer." δέησις (deêsis), 1162. Root from 1189a δέομαι (deomai) "ask, beg, implore." With its roots in δέω (deo). "to tie, bind." NASB Dictionary.

[77] John 1:1-3 states of Jesus Christ; "In the beginning was the Word, and the Word was with God, and the Word was God. He was with God in the beginning. Through him all things were made; without him nothing was made that has been made." Colossians 1:15-17 adds, "He is the image of the invisible God, the firstborn over all creation. For by him all things were created: things in heaven and on earth, visible and invisible, whether thrones or powers or rulers or authorities; all things were created by him and for him. He is before all things, and in him all things hold together."

restored by Jesus! This is one of so many examples in the Bible where God blesses those who trust Him!

Perhaps he had remembered the prophet Jeremiah's words:

> *This is one of so many examples in the Bible where God blesses those who trust Him!*

> Blessed is the man who
> trusts in the Lord
> And whose trust is the Lord.
> For he will be like a tree
> planted by the water,
> That extends its roots by a stream
> And will not fear when the heat comes;
> But its leaves will be green,
> And it will not be anxious in a year of drought
> Nor cease to yield fruit. (Jeremiah 17:7-8, NASB)

Or maybe he recounted what Solomon wrote many years before; "Whoever gives heed to instruction prospers, and blessed is he who trusts in the Lord." (Proverbs 16:20) Either one, it is clear that we too need to adopt this pattern in our lives!

HIT:

Humble yourself,
Implore Jesus, and
Trust Him.

Growing Deeper...

▶ Examine your own life by comparing it to Jairus and his story. Are you humble like he was, or do you find yourself clinging to the world and its arrogant philosophy of placing self above all else?

▶ If you decide that you are not humble, what are you going to do about it?

▶ Have you implored Jesus for anything lately?

▶ Are you trusting Jesus for the important things in your life?

The Bible to Life

Chapter 12

ACTS that Lead to Peace

Acknowledge God,
Call out to Him,
Thank Him, and
Share requests with Him.

A stressed businessman at the height of busyness quipped, "I've got so much to worry about, if something else comes up, it's gonna take me two weeks to get to it."

Another worried man said to a friend, "I'll give you $1000 to do my worrying for me." The friend replied, "Sounds great to me, when you going to pay me?" The first man responded, "Well that's the first thing you've got to worry about."

Tons of worry, stress and anxiety abound today, and to be clear, it is negative stress we are concerned about since positive stress is beneficial, leading to productivity and fulfillment. Positive stress is what we experience when exercising, playing sports, or meeting new people. Negative stress on the other hand, leads to anxiety and poor emotional, mental, social and physical health.

According to a Gallup poll, about eight in 10 Americans (79%) say they frequently (44%) or sometimes (35%) encounter negative stress in their daily lives. Just 17% say they rarely feel stressed, while 4% say they never do.[78]

The symptoms of stress are irritability, anger, nervousness, anxiousness, lack of interest and motivation, fatigue, and overwhelming feelings, like sadness and depression. The most common stress reducers are surfing the internet, watching TV and movies, sleeping, eating, drinking alcohol, using drugs, and smoking. The problem with these options is that they do not bring lasting relief, only temporary ease of symptoms.

Anxiety is a leading cause of stress and is defined by the American Psychological Association (APA) as "an emotion characterized by feelings of tension, worried thoughts and physical changes like increased blood pressure."[79] Anxiety is a normal and often healthy emotion, however, when a person regularly feels disproportionate levels of anxiety, it might become a medical disorder.

Anxiety disorders form a category of mental health diagnoses that lead to excessive nervousness, fear, apprehension, and worry. These disorders alter how a person processes emotions and behaves, also causing physical symptoms. Mild anxiety might be vague and unsettling, while severe anxiety may seriously affect day-to-day living.

According to the APA, anxiety disorders affect 40 million people in the United States. It is the most common group of mental illnesses in the country. However, only 36.9 percent of people with an anxiety disorder receive treatment.[80]

---

[78] December 20, 2017, https://news.gallup.com/poll/224336/eight-americans-afflicted-stress.aspx)

[79] https://www.medicalnewstoday.com/articles/323454.php

[80] Ibid.

In a Leadership Talk, John Maxwell asked the question, "Why worry?" Here's what he concluded about our worries:

40 percent will never happen.
30 percent concern old decisions that cannot be changed.
12 percent centers upon criticisms made by people who feel inferior.
10 percent are related to my health, which worsens when I worry.
8 percent are legitimate, which can be met head-on when I have eliminated senseless worries.

According to Philippians 4:4-9, one will find peace and overcome negative stress and anxiety through vigorous spiritual activities like **ACTS**. The cure is the peace of God "which transcends all understanding," and "will guard your hearts and your minds in Christ Jesus." But how do we get this peace? We can receive it by first finding Jesus Christ by knowing our **ABC's** (see chapter 1);

Admit that we are sinners,
Believe that Jesus Christ died on the cross in our place and paid the penalty for our sin, and
Confess that Jesus Christ is Lord.

Once we have done this, following the **ACTS** in Philippians 4:4-9 will cure our anxiety:

Rejoice in the Lord always. I will say it again: Rejoice! Let your gentleness be evident to all. The Lord is near. Do not be anxious about anything, but in everything, by **prayer** (Acknowledge God) and **petition** (**C**all out), with **thanksgiving** (**T**hankfulness), **present** (**S**hare) your requests to God. And the peace of God, which transcends all understanding, will guard your hearts and your minds in Christ Jesus. Finally, brothers, whatever is true, whatever is noble, whatever is right, whatever is pure, whatever is lovely, whatever is admirable—if anything is excellent or praiseworthy—think about such things. Whatever you have learned or received or heard from me, or seen in me—put it into practice. And the God of peace will be with you.

The first step:

Acknowledge God.

The meaning of the word for "prayer" here has to do with praying to a God who is not only able to answer, but Who is also both nearby and worthy! He is the only One who can help us in our trials and need! In the Greek New Testament this word for prayer is a compound word mainly meaning, "make prayers, offer prayers" and "earnestly pray, worship."[81] You can see this worshipful acknowledgment in Paul's admonition to the church Timothy was pastoring; "I want men everywhere to lift up holy hands in prayer, without anger or disputing." (1 Timothy 2:8) Here worship and prayer are connected. Jesus used it similarly by joining acknowledgment and praise; "When you pray, say: 'Father, hallowed be your name, your kingdom come.'" (Luke 11:2)

---

[81] Prayer = "earnestly, place of prayer, prayer, prayers." προσευχή (proseuchê), 4335. Root: from 4336; προσεύχομαι (proseuchomai), = "to pray, make prayers, worship, pray earnestly for." 4336. Root: from πρός (pros) 4314 = "among, with, toward," and εὔχομαι (euchomai) 2172 = "pray, wish." NASB Concordance and Strong's Dictionary.

Call out to Him.

After acknowledging God's worthiness, we are told to "petition" Him for what we need. This word in the Greek New Testament means, "to entreaty, request" and has roots in the idea of wanting, asking and even begging![82] How often have you begged God to intervene in your or someone another person's situation?

When we petition the government, we sign our name in support of a specific cause urging elected officials to listen to our needs or demands. God encourages us to do the same with Him in our prayers. Remember the persistent widow Jesus told the disciples about? In Luke 18:1-6, He taught them that "...they should always pray and never give up" (v. 1) and that the widow wore out the judge with whom she sought justice (v. 5). He then pronounced, "And will not God bring about justice for his chosen ones, who cry out to him day and night? Will he keep putting them off?" (v. 7). The answer to this rhetorical question is obvious, He will not keep putting us off when we petition Him!

Acknowledge and Call out to God.

Thank God.

The famous radio preacher David Jeremiah quipped on thankfulness, "an attitude of gratitude sets the altitude." We will be in a much better place emotionally and spiritually when we thank God for what He has done! Psalms 105:1 proclaims, "Give thanks to the Lord, call on his name; make known among the nations what he has done."

---

[82] Petition = "entreaty, prayer, supplication, request." δέησις (deêsis),1162. Root: from 1189a; "to want, entreat, ask, beg." δέομαι (deomai). NASB Concordance.

We are encouraged many times in scripture to be thankful. One significant example is in Ephesians, "always giving thanks to God the Father for everything, in the name of our Lord Jesus Christ." (Ephesians 5:20) And from the Psalms, "I will give thanks to the Lord with all my heart; I will tell of all Your wonders." (Psalms 9:1, NASB) Thank God.

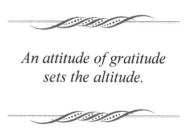

An attitude of gratitude sets the altitude.

Share Your Requests with God.

Take all your concerns to God. He cares for us deeply and is waiting to hear from us. Psalms 20:5 observes, "We will sing for joy over your victory, And in the name of our God we will set up our banners. May the Lord fulfill all your petitions." (NASB) In the throne room of God in Heaven, the 24 elders around the throne hold our prayers before the Lord; "And when he had taken it, the four living creatures and the twenty-four elders fell down before the Lamb. Each one had a harp and they were holding golden bowls full of incense, which are the **prayers of the saints**." (Revelation 5:8)

Here are some more Scriptures to consider:

Isaiah 30:15 "This is what the Sovereign Lord, the Holy One of Israel, says: 'In repentance and rest is your salvation, in quietness and trust is your strength…'"

Psalms 127:2 "In vain you rise early and stay up late, toiling for food to eat— for He grants sleep to those he loves." The NASB puts it this way; "It is vain for you to rise up early, To retire late, To eat the bread of painful labors; For He gives to His beloved *even in his* sleep."

Proverbs 3:1-6 "My son, do not forget my teaching, but keep my commands in your heart, for they will prolong your life many years and bring you prosperity.

Let love and faithfulness never leave you; bind them around your neck, write them on the tablet of your heart.

Then you will win favor and a good name in the sight of God and man.

Trust in the Lord with all your heart and lean not on your own understanding; in all your ways acknowledge him, and he will make your paths straight...."

Hebrews 5:7 "During the days of Jesus' life on earth, he offered up prayers and petitions with loud cries and tears to the one who could save him from death, and he was heard because of his reverent submission."

Throw Your Anxiety Away!

The apostle Peter told the churches in his day, and this is for us today as well, to literally throw away anxiety!

Therefore humble yourselves under the mighty hand of God, that He may exalt you at the proper time, **casting all your anxiety on Him, because He cares for you**. Be of sober spirit, be on the alert. Your adversary, the devil, prowls around like a roaring lion, seeking someone to devour. But resist him, firm in your faith, knowing that the same experiences of suffering are being accomplished by your brethren who are in the world. After you have suffered for a little while, the God of all grace, who called you to His eternal glory in Christ, will Himself perfect, confirm, strengthen and establish you. To Him be dominion forever and ever. Amen. (1 Peter 5:6-11, NASB)

God wants us to throw away our anxiety like we do the trash.

Note in verse 7 that "casting" literally means "throwing[83] your worries, anxiety or concerns[84] on Him because you matter to Him ("He cares for you" literally means "it matters concerning you" and "to be the object of His care"[85])! God wants us to throw away our anxiety like we do the trash. We don't want it anymore; we are tired of it and it stinks! It needs to go now! Can you do that? Can you leave your rubbish with Him and trust Him with it? Or do you want to keep hashing it over and over again, stressing yourself and those around you, and raising your blood pressure to dangerous levels? Get rid of it now, throw it away! There is no one who can handle your problems better than God. You can trust Him.

"And we know that in all things God works for the good of those who love him, who have been called according to his purpose." (Romans 8:28) Share your requests with Him.

ACTS:

Acknowledge God,
Call out to Him,
Thank Him, and
Share requests with Him.

---

[83] Cast = Ἐπιρίπτω = "cast upon or throw upon", 1977. NASB Concordance of the Bible.

[84] Anxiety = μέριμνα = "care, concern, anxiety, worries", 3308. Ibid.

[85] Cares = matters, concern, 3199. Ibid.

Growing Deeper...

▶ What trash or anxiety in your life is bothering you?

▶ Have you gotten so used to the stink that you like its familiarity? Why not throw it away?

▶ Can you trust God to handle your anxiety?

▶ Read Hebrews 5:7 over a few times. It informs us that *Jesus prayed with loud cries and tears* too, and was heard because of His submission! Note also the same numbers used in these references; "5:7". 1 Peter **5:7** (us) and Hebrews **5:7** (Jesus).

The Bible to Life

Chapter 13

PREP for Dangerous Times

Prioritize time with God,
Reserve time with God,
Enjoy time with God, and
Pick a Place for time with God.

For those of us who have a relationship with Jesus Christ, are part of a conservative evangelical Christian church and who seriously practice our faith, these are unprecedented and alarming days we live in!

A new study by Gallup, released in February of 2022, revealed that the numbers of those who identify in the LGBTQ+ community have risen by over 100% since 2012. This is a 26% increase since 2021, so now 7% of American adults self-identify as such! What's even more alarming, is that in the age group from 18 to 24, a whopping 39% are now self-identifying as part of the LGBTQ+ community! The answer given for the sharp increase is the impact of Hollywood's sexualization of viewers and the newfound fad of open and optional sexual experiences. With few of these young adults claiming to have been "born that way", this new and dangerous trend is pushing its way in on tattoos, body piercings and skinny jeans.[86]

---

[86] American Family Association Newsletter, 6/2/22, quoting a Gallup poll from February, and a World magazine article written by Joseph Backholm

The consequences for these decisions are mind-boggling. In 2015 the CDC reported that about 1/3 of all Americans suffered from STDs, but recently the CDC added, "STDs take a particularly heavy toll on young people. The CDC estimates that youth ages 15-24 account for almost half of the 26 million new sexually transmitted infections that occurred in the United States in 2018.[87] We used to be warned about these dangers, now we are encouraged to foolishly dive into them. In the world of substance abuse, "Fentanyl has driven an ever-worsening opioid crisis that killed over 100,000 Americans in 2021, more than suicides, car accidents or gun violence."[88] An estimated 109,680 people died in the U.S. in 2022.[89] There has been a growing trend to encourage "controlled use" rather than getting addicts clean! Recently a New York City poster ad read, "Don't be ashamed you are using, be empowered that you are using safely,"[90] New York City, a leader of the controversial "harm reduction" approach to drug addiction, opened the country's first officially authorized injection sites in November. Worse still, the Biden administration has apparently started funding the distribution of crack pipes as part of a $30 billion "harm-reduction program".[91]

For me, as someone who has spent many years in pastoral ministry and Biblical higher education, the stats regarding pastors

---

of the Family Research Council.

[87] https://www.cdc.gov/std/life-stages-populations/adolescents-youngadults.htm

[88] https://redwhiteblueinbox.com/articles/quote-of-the-day-drug-addiction-can-be-empowering

[89] https://blogs.cdc.gov/nchs/2023/05/18/7365/.

[90] Ibid.

[91] https://freebeacon.com/biden-administration/yes-safe-smoking-kits-include-free-crack-pipes-we-know-because-we-got-them/

is far more dangerous and concerning! A recent poll by George Barna reveals that just 37% of all Christian pastors in the United States have a biblical worldview. Only 51% of evangelical pastors in the United States have a biblical worldview and just 57% of conservative evangelical pastors have a biblical worldview.[92]

The Merriam Webster dictionary defines worldview as "a comprehensive conception of the world, especially from a specific standpoint." In other words, it is a collection of all the information a person has heard, watched, and learned from all sources like parents, teachers, preachers, TV, movies, friends and relatives in their small part of the world. The more someone has learned and traveled, the bigger their worldview becomes. To hold a biblical worldview is to have a view of the world that is understood through the lens of scripture. The Bible being the standard and authority by which all of one's ethical and moral decisions are made and practiced. The more one studies and practice its teachings, the stronger his or her biblical worldview. And for pastors and preachers, it includes what they are teaching and training their congregations.

Let's look at this from the other side. These numbers tell us that 6 out of 10 Christian pastors in the U.S. do not have a biblical worldview and do not use the Bible for their standard of measuring ethical and moral decisions! 5 out of 10 evangelical pastors in the United States do not have a biblical worldview, and an unbelievable 4 out of 10 conservative evangelical pastors do not hold to a biblical worldview! It is no wonder our governments and universities have dropped a biblical or Christian worldview, just as the church in America has!

---

[92] Family Research Council, *Spiritual Shepherds Not Flocking to Word of God* by Joshua Arnold, 5/27/22.

This poses a tremendous challenge for and threat to the Church of Jesus Christ today, because pastors are shepherds for the Church under our Great Shepherd Jesus Christ! Sheep need shepherds to guide them since they are dumb and blindly follow their shepherd. Good shepherds take care of their sheep and guide them to where they will be well fed, watered, and protected. Bad shepherds, however, don't provide such good care and don't even mind losing some sheep along the way.

If sheep have no shepherd, then they will simply follow the herd, even to the point of running off a cliff! This is precisely what is happening to so many blinded people in our culture today, especially young people! Today we need good shepherds for our churches and our communities and our young people! Will you be a good shepherd? Even if you're not called to be the senior shepherd of a church, will you be a faithful and good shepherd? Will you choose to do the ministry you are called to from a biblical worldview vantage point?

Jesus said "my sheep hear my voice and follow me." Followers of Jesus Christ, like sheep, need a leader, and most people follow one who they think is good, not one necessarily who is good, holy, and Christlike. Their understanding of what is good is based on their worldview, which as we have seen, may be far from biblical! Even in the church, many people are led astray by pastors and leaders who do not have a biblical worldview!

Typically, the maximum life of a church is about 80 years and at the 40-year mark churches start to make poor decisions and to decline. They can be revitalized, but most often they are not, and they decline very rapidly because they make perceived moral choices rather than careful and prayerful biblical choices. They start to talk about God rather than God the Father, God the

Son, and God the Holy Spirit. Jesus and the Holy Spirit usually are the first to go. Even in the United States government, the 13 colonies started out strong by following "the Divine Sovereign. the Lord Jesus Christ."[93] In 1953 the trend continued when Congress established the motto "In God We Trust". Just a few years ago President Obama said the U.S. was not a Christian nation anymore, and allowed a Congressman to be sworn in with a Koran. Now, "God" is defined totally by individual choice, by one's own worldview. Why? Because we are so influenced by our culture, or should I say the world? If we love the world according to the apostles James (chapter 4) and John (1 Jn 2), we become enemies of God.

Let's read 1 John chapter 2:15-17, and the following verses:

> Do not love the world or anything in the world. If anyone loves the world, the love of the Father is not in him. For everything in the world—the cravings of sinful man ("lust of the flesh", man's sinful human nature = addictions), the lust of his eyes (materialism, coveting, jealousy) and the boasting of what he has and does (pride in one's self. These are 3 root sins from which other sins sprout)—comes not from the Father but from the world. The world and its desires pass away, but the man who does the will of God lives forever.

> James 4:4 adds, "You adulterous people, don't you know that friendship with the world is hatred toward God? Anyone who chooses to be a friend of the world becomes an enemy of God."

---

[93] *America's God and Country*, William Federer, p. 143, Fame Publishing.

So the obvious question arises, how can we avoid becoming an enemy of God? How can we stand against such powerful enemies like the world, Satan and demons, and our own flesh? We must learn to PREP for ministry like Jesus did. Mark 1:35 says that "Very early in the morning, while it was still dark, Jesus got up, left the house, and went off to a solitary place where he prayed." We must do the same! Let me suggest a few practical principles that Jesus himself applied. We will remember this better with the acronym **PREP:**

Prioritize time with God.

"Very early in the morning, while it was still dark..." Martin Luther, when speaking about a full plate or responsibilities, is reported to have said, "I have so much to do each day that I must spend the first 3 hours in prayer."[94] He wisely followed Jesus' example and was used by God to bring about great reform in the Church!

In 1952 a doctoral student at Princeton University asked Albert Einstein what original idea was there left to research, and Einstein replied, "Find out about prayer. Somebody must find out about prayer."[95] Even for Einstein there was a need to discover the importance and power of prayer.

Reserve time with God.

According to Luke 5:16, Jesus "often withdrew to lonely places to pray." In "My Utmost for his Highest", J. Oswald Sanders wrote, "prayer does not equip us for greater works — prayer

---

[94] Frank Minrith, You Can! 7 Principles for Winning in Life, p. 63. Nelson Publishing, 1994.

[95] Ibid., p. 64.

is the greater work." Reserving time with God fosters more prayer, which in turn enables greater work to happen for Christ's kingdom.

Enjoy time with God.

Psalms 27:8 proclaims, "My heart says of you, 'Seek his face!' Your face, Lord, I will seek." And about the Bible, Psalms 119:103 says, "How sweet are your words to my taste, sweeter than honey to my mouth!" God's word is not just necessary for growth, it is enjoyable and rewarding!

Pick a Place for time with God.

In Matthew 6, Jesus warned about praying before men just to be seen by them, and suggested we pray in our room or "closet" as the King James Version reads. He wants us to spend personal time with Him. As we have already noted, Jesus set an example for us as He often found solitary places to pray.

Back to James 4. Note that verse 8 provides a fabulous principle to closeness with God our Father and maintaining a solid biblical worldview: "Draw near to God and He will draw near to you." Will you draw near to God? Will you develop and maintain a healthy biblical worldview? Will you be a good shepherd? Will you be an influencer for Jesus Christ? Rather than being social media influencers, we must become biblical media influencers!

Rather than being social media influencers, we must become biblical media influencers!

PREP:

Prioritize time with God,
Reserve time with God,
Enjoy time with God, and
Pick a Place for time with God.

Growing Deeper...

▶ Do you feel you are ready for these difficult times we live in?

▶ Have you made it a priority in your life to spend time alone with the heavenly Father?

▶ What steps have you taken to ensure a place and time for the Lord? If not yet, take some time right now to make some goals and plans to make it happen.

▶ Remember, God said in James 4:8, "Draw near to Me and I will draw near to you."

The Bible to Life

Chapter 14

The Original GPS

Godly
Positioning
System

The GPS we use today in our cars and phones are Global Positioning Systems. They help us to navigate to where we want to go by inputting our departure and arrival locations, and by following their specified directions, they help us navigate safely and timely.

The GPS most of us use has an aerial view or satellite view of the ground or a map, helping us to see where we are going as we travel. But there are other types of GPS as well. There is one for airplanes which gives pilots a forward or a cross-section view of what's ahead. This is necessary so airplanes don't run into mountains, towers, and other planes. Another type of GPS is one that is used on bulldozers and road graders. It is similar to the forward or cross section view in that it aids the bulldozer or road grader operator to cut dirt off of high spots and fill it into low spots while building a road. There is even a more expensive and more sophisticated system that can be used on these machines that is fully automated. What incredible advances in engineering and technology these are!

The original GPS, however, was given to us by God to navigate life well, and we call it the Holy Bible. Another name for it would be the **G**odly **P**ositioning **S**ystem. It is a great gift enabling us to find our way spiritually and to grow in a relationship with God.

The original GPS was given to us by God to navigate life well.

It was written by over 40 authors, from different walks of life over a 1500-year period, and yet reads as one book with one author, which is of course God the Father, with one main subject—Jesus Christ (Messiah) His Son.[96]

God's GPS is Godly in two ways. First, it provides God's guidelines or rules of the road for us to follow. Secondly, it reveals God's example to us. Ephesians 5:18 encourages us to "be imitators of God…"

Psalm 119 is a fascinating chapter about the Bible and informs us in great detail about it. Of the 1189 chapters in the Bible, it is the longest[97], is in the center of the Bible[98], and is entirely about the Bible! It is written in Hebrew poetic form with 22 sections of eight verses each, with each section starting with a letter of the Hebrew alphabet in alphabetical order. In fact, the first two letters of the Hebrew alphabet (Old Testament) are aleph and beth (sounds like bate) and the first two letters of the Greek alphabet (New Testament) are alpha and beta. This is where our

---

[96] Christ is the English for Christos in Greek, which is the same as Messiah in English from the Hebrew Mashiach meaning "anointed one." NASB Concordance.

[97] Psalm 117 is the shortest chapter of the Bible.

[98] Psalm 118 is the actual center chapter of the Bible.

English word "alphabet" originated from, by combining these first two letters alpha + beta = alphabet.[99]

There are eight important words in this chapter which are descriptive of the many names and forms of God's word[100] and they are used in all but 7 of the 176 verses. The first word is "law". It's the same word in Hebrew for Torah which means "direction, instruction."

The second word is "testimony", and it means "admonition, ordinance or statute." This would be a testimony where one is not talking about what God or someone else has done, but rather one where the person admonishes others to whom he is speaking. The third word is "commandment"[101] and it is defined as "an order given" such as is practiced in the military, like when a commanding officer shouts, "Drop and give me fifty!"

Another similar word like commandment is the word "precept."[102] It is defined as "a command intended, especially as a rule of action." This common biblical word refers to instructions from God that are intended to be on-going in a believer's life. The fifth word, is the word "statute." This refers to "something prescribed or owed." Just as a doctor prescribes drugs and actions one can take to become healthy physically, God

---

[99] "The word *alphabet* comes from the first two letters of the Greek alphabet: alpha and beta. It was first used, in its Latin form, *alphabetum*, by Tertullian during the 2nd–3rd century CE and by St. Jerome. The Classical Greeks customarily used the plural of *to gramma* ("the letter"); the later form *alphabētos* was probably adopted under Latin influence." https://www.britannica.com/question/Where-does-the-word-alphabet-come-from.

[100] New American Standard Hebrew Lexicon of the Bible and Strong's Hebrew Lexicon.

[101] Ibid.

[102] Merriam Webster Dictionary.

prescribes teachings in Scripture that will help us grow spiritually, emotionally, and even physically at times.

The next word is "judgment." This relates to "justice and ordinances". When a judge pronounces a judgment, he is directing the path of the sentenced convict. The seventh word is "word" which has to do with "speech and words." And the final one is "promise", defined as "word" as in "I give you my word."

4 Things You Want from a GPS

First, *you want to know it works.* Psalms 119:98-100 states that it will indeed succeed, "Your commands make me wiser than my enemies, for they are ever with me. I have more insight than all my teachers, for I meditate on your statutes. I have more understanding than the elders, for I obey your precepts."

I have experienced having "more insight than all my teachers" on more than one occasion. When I was in the eighth grade, my atheist science teacher attempted to tell our class that God did not create the world, rather scientists believed in evolutionary origins without a Creator. Just prior to this, God had called me to full time ministry, so He emboldened me to disagree with the learned teacher. After the fireworks settled, I managed to pass the class anyway. A few years later I met that teacher in church and discovered he had changed his views entirely as he had become a believer too and married into a great Christian family! Could it be that an emboldened teen had more truth than his teacher because of his interaction with the word of God and consequently became part of a complete intellectual and spiritual makeover for his instructor?

The statement "I have more understanding than the elders..." may not make sense to us today, as many people simply ask

Siri or they "Google" the information they need. In ancient cultures and even in times not too far back from us, knowledge of specific categories was held only by libraries and wise people. "Elders" were such people who were older and possessed life experience. Our ancestors relied on the wisdom of those who had gone before us to live successfully. Even while "...the honor of old men is their gray hair" (Proverbs 20:29, NASB), the believer who obeys God's word will have more understanding than them!

The second benefit you want from your GPS, is *you want to know how to get where you are going*. Psalms 119:105 informs that God's word provides direction and protection, "Your word is a lamp to my feet and a light for my path." The oil lamps in use when this passage was written were small enough to hold in the palm of a hand and gave a small flame of light about an inch or two high, much like a Bic lighter today. The holder of the lamp could only see a few feet ahead, just enough to not stumble and fall, "a lamp to my feet" (protection) and just enough light to find his way, "a light for my path" (direction).

Thirdly, *you want to have a safe trip*. Psalms 119:101 declares, "I have kept my feet from every evil path so that I might obey your word." Psalms 119:11 adds, "I have hidden your word in my heart that I might not sin against you." Sin brings with it consequences like shame, guilt, pain and suffering, but the one who obeys God's word will be safe.

Finally, *you want to enjoy your journey*. Psalms 119:103 reveals that you certainly will enjoy your trip if you invest in time with your Bible, "How sweet are your words to my taste, sweeter than honey to my mouth!" Dates grew wildly all over Israel and were used to make honey. It was the sweetest tasting food one could put in his mouth at that time and place, and the Psalmist wrote that the word of God was sweeter! Isaiah exclaimed something very similar, "The steadfast of mind You will keep in perfect peace, because he trusts in You." (Isaiah 26:3, NASB).

Vicente' was an African witch doctor who one day noticed a serious moral decline in his community. After pondering for several weeks what to do, he decided to travel to the nearest city and find a religious bookstore to see if he could purchase a holy book that might direct him to a solution. He bought one and brought it back to his village and began reading it to his friends and family. Soon, nearly everyone from the community was attending his readings, and he began to see moral changes and improvements in his tribe.

A Christian missionary who happened to be in the area heard about the well-attended meetings and investigated them. To his amazement and delight, he discovered the villagers had become believers in Jesus Christ and a church had been planted! The holy book Vicente' had purchased was a "Holy Bible"!

The original GPS helped a whole village get to where they needed to be. It can help anyone and everyone who will pick it up and use it.

GPS

Godly
Positioning
System

Growing Deeper...

▶ What is your personal navigational system?

▶ How is it working out for you?

▶ Are you ready to give God's Positioning System a go?

The Bible to Life

Chapter 15

The Biblical Education TEST

Teach the Bible,
Expose Error,
Straighten Doctrine, and
Train Disciples.

" All Scripture is inspired by God and profitable for **teaching**, for **reproof**, for **correction**, for **training** in righteousness; so that the man of God may be adequate, equipped for every good work. 2 Timothy 3:16-17 (NASB)

When studying 2 Timothy 3:16 a little while back, I decided to do word studies on the four key words Paul uses when he's talking about the educational and spiritual "profit" of God's word. Not only was I intrigued by the acronym **TEST** that came from the four words, but I discovered the words were actually levels to learning, like climbing steps on the biblical education staircase.

Teach the Bible.

The first step a student takes on their journey is learning from "teaching" or "instruction, conveying information" by speaking truth. The Greek word is *didaskalos* from where we get the English word "didactic"[103] and means, "designed or intended to teach: intended to convey instruction and information as well as pleasure and entertainment." In Matthew 28:19-20 Jesus commissioned His disciples; "Therefore go and make disciples of all nations, baptizing them in the name of the Father and of the Son and of the Holy Spirit, and **teaching** them to obey everything I have commanded you. And surely I am with you always, to the very end of the age." Truth is first discovered from its teaching.

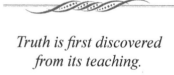

Truth is first discovered from its teaching.

Expose Error.

The second word "reproof" or "rebuke" takes us up another step in our spiritual growth journey by commanding that we deal with error in our thinking as well. A good translation of this word is "to expose."[104] So we are not to only teach truth, but we must expose error or untruths as well. In Matthew 7:5 (NASB) Jesus challenged believers about judging and exposing error; "You hypocrite, first take the log out of your own eye, and then you will see clearly to take the speck out of your brother's eye." Again in 1 Corinthians 11:31, Paul followed Christ's lead and encouraged the church in Corinth to evaluate themselves carefully and avoid future judgment, "For if we would judge ourselves, we would not be judged."

---

[103] Defined as "designed or intended to teach people something." https://www.britannica.com/dictionary/didactic. NASB Concordance.

[104] "Reproof" in NASB, NRSV, ESV, NKJV, and KJV is elegmos, with root elegchô = "exposing, convicting." Ibid.

Straighten Doctrine.

The third Greek word has the root *orthosis*[105] where we get the English transliteration "ortho" as in orthodontist or orthopedic, for "straightening" teeth and limbs. So we as Bible teachers should help guide a student's doctrine and worldview through proper exegesis[106] (interpretation of the text),[107] to be straightly aligned with Scripture and God's leading in our lives. In 2 Timothy 4:2 Paul uses this same word as he demands Timothy pastor his sheep (people) carefully, "Preach the Word; be prepared in season and out of season; **correct**, rebuke and encourage—with great patience and careful instruction."

Train Disciples.

The final word in this intriguing and instructive verse is "training." It comes from the Greek word *paideuo* meaning "to train children, discipline, punish."[108] Those of us who have raised chil-

---

[105] Correcting (all translations are the same here). ἐπανόρθωσις/epan-**orthôsis**, root ἀνορθόω/anorthoô = "to set straight again, from orthoô = "to set straight or Straightening". Ibid.

[106] Lit. to get "the meaning out of" the text, like an exit gets one out of a building. "Theological scholars have long been preoccupied with interpreting the meanings of various passages in the Bible. In fact, because of the sacred status of the Bible in both Judaism and Christianity, biblical interpretation has played a crucial role in both of those religions throughout their histories. English speakers have used the word *exegesis*—a descendant of the Greek term *exēgeisthai*, meaning "to explain" or "to interpret"—to refer to explanations of Scripture since the early 17th century. Nowadays, however, academic writers interpret all sorts of texts, and *exegesis* is no longer associated mainly with the Bible." https://www.merriam-webster.com/dictionary/ exegesis.

[107] See chapter 16, 4 Simple Steps to READ Your Bible Better.

[108] "Instruction" in NKJV and KJV. παιδεία/paideia = lit. "the rearing of a child, training, discipline", root παιδεύω/paideuô = "to train children,

dren know full well how much time, effort and other resources go into training them, whether or not we are successful at it. In 1 Timothy 4:7 church leaders are also encouraged to train themselves, "Have nothing to do with godless myths and old wives' tales; rather, **train** yourself to be godly." Sadly, these last two steps of straightening and training are rarely part of a church's educational or discipleship ministry.

Verse 17 provides us with the wonderful results of this TEST, that the "...man of God may be thoroughly equipped for every good work." The New Testament definition of "thoroughly" is "fitted, complete, adequate"[109] and the definition of "equipped" is "to complete, to equip fully" from a root word meaning "get ready, prepare." The individual that completes the Bible TEST steps will be completely equipped and prepared for every good work![110]

Training
Straightening
Exposing
Teaching

---

to chasten, correct, discipline, punish [e.g. military training]." NASB Concordance.

[109] ἄρτιος/artios = "fitted, complete, adequate." Root from αρτίζω/artizô = "get ready, prepare." Ibid.

[110] "Every good work", ἔργον/ergon = "action, behavior, deed." Ibid.

The Biblical Education TEST

Teach the Bible,
Expose error,
Straighten doctrine, and
Train disciples.

Growing Deeper...

▶ Is your doctrine straight/correct?

▶ Do you know how to catch or detect error in preaching and teaching?

▶ Is your church or small group aware of the 4 steps and practicing them?

127

The Bible to Life

Chapter 16

4 Simple Steps to READ
Your Bible Better

Research,
Evaluation,
Application, and
Devotion.

According to pollster George Gallup, 3 out of 4 Americans believe the Bible to be the actual or inspired word of God![111] While this is an encouraging find, less than half of these believers are reading the Bible daily or weekly, which equals one third of all Americans.[112] Reading the Bible more is great and beneficial, but how well are we reading, interpreting and understanding it? Have you ever thought to yourself, "I read it, but I didn't get it?"

Here is a simple four-step plan to help us "get it", to help us understand and interpret the Bible better, based on the acronym **READ**:

Research.

The first step is found in the first letter "**R**", which stands for **Research.** We must research or make "an extensive

---

[111] http://news.gallup.com/poll/170834/three-four-bible-word-god.aspx

[112] https://www.barna.com/research/the-bible-in-america-6-year-trends/

investigation"[113] into the Word of God. We are implored by 2 Timothy 2:15 to "Be diligent to present yourself approved to God as a workman who does not need to be ashamed, accurately handling the word of truth."[114] In order for us to "accurately handle" the Bible, we must understand and apply three rules to reading it right; **context, context, context!** Sound familiar? Much like the three rules of real estate (location, location, location), context holds the greatest value in unlocking the meaning of the biblical text! Once we know the proper context of a biblical passage, we have or are very close to having the primary meaning of the text we are studying. Context is defined as "the parts of a written or spoken statement that precede or follow a specific word or passage, usually influencing its meaning or effect."[115]

Context holds the greatest value in unlocking the meaning of the biblical text!

The way to find the context of a single verse is to read the whole chapter before concluding the verse's meaning. The greater context is the book or letter itself, and then the whole Bible for the big picture (chronological Bibles are great for this), where you compare passages that say the same or similar thing. Reading other translations is also very helpful in providing understanding as they may use words and phrases that are more familiar to us. Avoid studying from paraphrases or non-translations (e.g. The Living Bible).

---

[113] http://www.dictionary.com/browse/research

[114] All Bible verses are quoted in the NASB unless otherwise noted.

[115] https://www.dictionary.com/browse/context

To make our reading more effective, we need to learn to **focus.** When we focus on the passage in front of us and ignore all distractions around us and in our minds, we can zero in on our reading. Sometimes it takes a lot of discipline, but it is well worth the effort when we see the results and we begin to truly understand the passage we are studying, and even better—hear God speak!

There are many tools today that we can use to help us get more from the biblical text. The most well-known one is the concordance, which is an alphabetical listing of all Bible verses using a specific word. Most concordances also have numbers linking them to the original Hebrew and Greek words which have definitions in the back of the book or in companion book called a lexicon. If you find a word in a verse that you don't understand or you think may mean more than its face value, this will help you understand the passage better and hopefully unlock its primary meaning. Computer software does this more easily; as simply as double clicking on the word you want (e.g. Logos, Wordsearch, Biblesoft). There are also websites like Biblehub.com and Netbible.org and apps like Blue Letter Bible that offer the same tools for free.

A topical Bible is another tool that helps immensely when you are doing a topical Bible study by providing a biblical outline of the subject matter. Add to this a Bible dictionary, which as you guessed, is a dictionary of biblical people, places, and events. Bible encyclopedias, handbooks and atlases provide much supportive information in the areas their names suggest. Bible commentaries are listed last because it is far better for the Bible student to read them after they have some sense of the interpretation of the passage, particularly since commentators generally provide it, but their conclusions often vary drastically!

Ask a mature believer who you trust to offer some direction on good commentaries like Warren Wiersbe's Bible Exposition Commentaries.

A good Study Bible has some or many of these tools included (e.g. The NIV Study Bible by Zondervan, also available in other translations), although some are often abridged too much.

Evaluation.

The next step is to **Evaluate** the information you've discovered. Bible teachers normally call this the interpretation phase. Here we want to sift through the information from our observations of the biblical passage and funnel it all down to determine what it meant to the original readers and hearers, and then what it means to us today, both personally and corporately (the church).

When discussing personal examination in preparation for the Lord's Supper, the apostle Paul gave us an insightful heads-up about God's judgment of us and our opportunity to avoid it—"But if we judged ourselves rightly, we would not be judged. 32 But when we are judged, we are disciplined by the Lord so that we will not be condemned along with the world. (1 Corinthians 11:31-32) Further, 2 Timothy 3:16-17 says, "All Scripture is inspired by God and profitable for teaching, for reproof, for correction, for training in righteousness; 17 so that the man of God may be adequate, [thoroughly] equipped for every good work."

Application.

The "A" in the acronym reminds us of the necessity to **Apply** what we have learned. James 1:22 says, "Do not merely listen to the Word, and so deceive yourselves. Do what it says." (NIV)

James 4:17 adds, "Anyone, then, who knows the good he ought to do and doesn't do it, sins."

One additional practice that helps immensely with research, evaluation, and application is **memorization.** Before the invention of the printing press, the Bible and all things written, were copied meticulously by hand or memorized and passed on orally. Psalm 119:15-16 says, "I will meditate on Your precepts, And contemplate Your ways. I will delight myself in Your statutes; I will not forget Your word." (NKJV) Psalm 119:11 adds "Your Word I have hidden in my heart that I might not sin against you." (NKJV) And Jesus said, "Apart from Me, you can do nothing." (John 15:5b) Here are three practical ways we can use our God-given **RAM:**

Repetition–repeat a phrase often and you will remember it.
Association–line up a new thought with something familiar.
Meditation–think carefully and much about what God said.

For more on memorizing Scripture, see Chapter 19, "RAM and SDRAM, A Bible Memory Plan".

Devotion.

Finally, **Devote** yourself to regular and continual research, evaluation, and application, and of course, prayer! This is where the idea of "devotions" comes from, that Christians all over the world commit to daily. James charged us with a promise to "Draw near to God, and He will draw near to you." (James 4:8) A little accountability goes a long way too. Ask someone for help and encouragement, "But encourage one another day after day, as long as it is still called "Today," so that none of you will be hardened by the deceitfulness of sin." (Hebrews 3:13) Also, "Let us not give up meeting together, as some are in the habit of doing, but let us encourage one another—and all the more as you see the Day approaching." (Hebrews 10:25)

READ:

Research,
Evaluation,
Application, and
Devotion.

Growing Deeper...

▶ Some practical advice on making your reading count:

1. Make brackets with your pen to the left side of the column where you have discovered information that has impacted you and note it that way. I prefer this to highlighting as you only need a pen and do not have to switch between a pen and a highlighter.

2. Write brief notes in front of your books about the sections you bracketed with the page number. This becomes a reference tool for you in the future when you need to recall the information.

3. Keep all the really good and helpful books you have invested time in, as you will need them in the future as you teach and disciple others.

4. Keep files and notes (and/or electronic files) of what you have gathered as you are researching. Again, this will be incredibly helpful to you down the road.

5. Put notes on your cellphone or other devices and back them up. They are especially easy to share with others. One suggestion that makes this easier is to use your microphone function on your smart phone to speak into your notepad what you have learned. You can then email the information to your computer for further file editing and cataloging.

▶ Spend some time looking over these great apps and websites for doing biblical research and explore a topic or a passage of interest to you:

www.blueletterbible.org
www.netbible.org
www.biblestudytools.com
www.gotquestions.org
www.biblehub.com

Bible study software:

www.logos.com (and now Wordsearch)
www.biblesoft.com

Some excellent books on bible study:

Living by the Book by Howard G. and William D. Hendricks (Chicago: Moody Press, 2007). *Handbook for Personal Bible Study* by William W. Klein (Colorado Springs: NavPress, 2008). *How to Study your Bible* by Kay Arthur (Eugene: Harvest House Publishers, 2014).
Pleasure and Profit in Bible Study by D.L. Moody (Chicago: Moody Press).

Some very good study Bibles:

The NASB Study Bible (Grand Rapids: Zondervan Publishing House, 1996).

The NIV Study Bible (Grand Rapids: Zondervan Publishing House, 1985).
The HCSB Study Bible (Nashville: Holman Bible Publishers, 2010).
The Archaeological Study Bible, NIV (Grand Rapids: Zondervan Publishing House, 2005).

A sampling of some other Bible study tools:

The Bible Background Commentary, New Testament. Keener, Craig S. Downers Grove: InterVarsity Press, 1993.

The Bible Background Commentary, Old Testament. John Walton. Downers Grove: InterVarsity Press, 2000.

Rose Book of Bible Charts, Maps & Timelines. Torrance: Rose Publishing, 2005.

Smith's Bible Dictionary. Smith, William. Nashville: Thomas Nelson Publishers, 1962.

Mounce's Complete Expository Dictionary of Old and New Testament Words. Mounce, William D. Grand Rapids: Zondervan Publishing House, 2006.

Exhaustive Concordance of the Bible. Strong, Augustus. Iowa Falls: World Bible Publishers, 1989.

The Bible Answer Book. Torrey, R.A. New Kensington: Whitaker House, 1999.

The New Topical Textbook. Torrey, R.A. Minneapolis: World Wide Publications.

Eerdmans Handbook to the Bible. Alexander, David and Alexander, Pat. Grand Rapids; Lion Publishing with Eerdmans Publishing, 1992.

The Wiersbe Bible Commentary, 2 Volumes, by Warren W. Wiersbe. Colorado Springs: David C. Cook Publishing, 2007.

The Complete Book of Everyday Christianity. Banks, Robert and Stevens, R. Paul. Downers Grove: InterVarsity Press, 1997.

The New International Dictionary of New Testament Theology. Brown, Colin, ed. Grand Rapids: Zondervan Publishing House, 1976.

Amazing Discoveries that Unlock the Bible. Connelly, Douglas. Grand Rapids: Zondervan Publishing House, 2008.

New Bible Dictionary. Douglas, J.D., ed. Leicester: Inter-Varsity Press, 1962.

The Complete Who's Who in the Bible. Gardner, Paul D., ed. Grand Rapids: Zondervan Publishing House, 1995.

Hard Sayings of the Bible. Kaiser, Walter C. Jr., Davids H. Peters, Bruce, F.F. and Brauch, Manfred T. Downers Grove: InterVarsity Press, 1996.

The Facts on the King James Only Debate. Ankerberg, John and Weldon, John. Eugene: Harvest House Publishers, 1996

The Bible to Life

Chapter 17

The One Who READs; **GROWS**

Get to know God,
Reveal truth,
Obey Him,
Walk in God's will, and be
Satisfied.

To begin this chapter, let's consider an analogy to link this
chapter with the last one. If you wish to make a tasty pie,
you will **R**esearch cookbooks, magazines and recipes on the web
and talk with other bakers you know who are good at baking.
Then you **E**valuate the recipes by reading and listening to what
others have said about them and compare them to similar ones.
Next you **A**pply the information you have gathered by putting
on an apron and measuring and mixing ingredients and baking
them off as directed. As you **D**evote yourself to more baking in
the kitchen, you will soon be able to end up with delightful des-
erts and tasty treats that you and others can enjoy, and, as we all
know, the more you practice, the better baker you will become.

In church on Sunday morning, the pastor spreads out a deli-
cious banquet with many good and tasty foods for everyone to
enjoy and have their fill. Everyone leaves the building spiritually
well fed and ready for the week ahead. But what happens later
in the day and the rest of the week? Everyone inevitably will
get hungry again and need to eat again. The pastor cannot feed

his flock three square meals a day, so who will do it? Believers must feed themselves; they must learn to bake (READ) for themselves! The secret is that the follower of Jesus who **READs. GROWS!** And opportunities will abound to:

Get to Know God.

First John 2:3-6 makes it very clear that knowing God starts with learning and obeying Him, "We know that *we have come to know him if we obey his commands.* The man who says, 'I know him,' but does not do what he commands is a liar, and the truth is not in him. But *if anyone obeys his word, God's love is truly made complete in him.* This is how we *know* we are in him: Whoever claims to live in him must walk as Jesus did." Hosea 4:6 adds that knowledge is extremely important for God's people, "My people are destroyed for lack of knowledge..."

Reveal Truth.

First John also informs us of the need for truth, "Dear friends, *do not believe every spirit,* but *test the spirits* to see whether they are from God, because many false prophets have gone out into the world." (4:1) Hebrews 4:12-13 adds the fact that God's word is penetrating and revealing,

> For the word of God is living and active. Sharper than any double-edged sword, it *penetrates even to dividing soul and spirit,* joints and marrow; it judges the thoughts and attitudes of the heart. Nothing in all creation is hidden from God's sight. Everything is uncovered and laid bare before the eyes of him to whom we must give account.

In the next chapter of Hebrews, constant use of God's word is responsible for maturing His children, "Anyone who lives on milk, being still an infant, is not acquainted with the teaching about righteousness. But *solid food is for the mature*, who by *constant use have trained themselves* to distinguish good from evil." (5:13-14) As indicated by the following quote, Mark Twain would likely have agreed, it is reported that he quipped, "It is not that people have learned too little, it is that they have learned too much that ain't so!"

Obey God.

Obedience has already been mentioned, but Psalms 119:101-102 solidifies the importance of it, "I have kept my feet from every evil path so that I might obey your word. I have not departed from your laws, for you yourself have taught me." Jesus reinforced this in John 14:23 when He replied, "If anyone loves me, he will obey my teaching. My Father will love him, and we will come to him and make our home with him."

Walk in God's Will.

Every believer at some point or maybe even many times in their walk with Christ asks questions about God's will for their lives. Psalms 119:105 provides us with helpful instruction as to the value of God's word in discovering it, "Your word is a lamp to my feet and a light to my path." The little flicker of light that emanated from the ancient middle eastern clay oil lamp was an illustration of how the Bible offers just enough light for our protection ("to my feet") and direction ("to my path").

Ephesians 5:17-21 offers further direction revealing God's righteous or moral will;

Therefore do not be foolish, but understand what the Lord's will is. Do not get drunk on wine, which leads to debauchery. Instead, be filled with the Spirit. Speak to one another with psalms, hymns and spiritual songs. Sing and make music in your heart to the Lord, always giving thanks to God the Father for everything, in the name of our Lord Jesus Christ.

Christ-like behavior is God's primary will for believers.

Satisfied. The French have a proverb; "A good meal ought to begin with hunger." It is hard to enjoy a meal when you are not yet hungry, but, when you are hungry, anything tastes good. If we approach the Word with a hunger to be filled, we will truly be satisfied every time. "The backslider in heart will have his fill of his own ways, But a good man will be satisfied with his" or "satisfied from above" as the New King James Version puts it (Proverbs 14:14, NASB). A psalmist expounded further about satisfaction from the word comparing the sweetest ingredient available to him, "How sweet are Your words to my taste, Sweeter than honey to my mouth!" (Psalms 119:103) Proverbs 14:14 adds that a reward is also forthcoming for good people, "The faithless will be fully repaid for their ways, and the good man rewarded for his."

Pablo Casals was considered the greatest cellist to ever live. When he was 95 years old, he was asked why he continued to practice 6 hours a day. He answered, "Because I think I'm making progress." Every disciple of Jesus Christ should learn from Casals and be committed and faithful for the progression of Christ's Kingdom on earth.

A group of tourists visiting a picturesque village walked by an old man sitting beside a fence. In a rather patronizing way, one tourist asked him, "Were any great men born in this village?" The old man replied, "Nope, only babies." Every person who is a born-again believer starts life as a baby in Christ. Whether the new convert is six or sixty, that person is still a new Christian and needs to grow in the Lord. A baby Christian who has been saved for forty years is a tragedy. God intends for us to grow and mature so that we can be a positive influence in the lives of others. Until we learn to dig into the meat of the word of God for ourselves, we will never grow up.

Are you a follower of Jesus Christ who **GROWS**?

God intends for us to grow and mature so that we can be a positive influence in the lives of others.

GROWS:

Get to know God,
Reveal truth,
Obey Him,
Walk in God's will, and be
Satisfied.

Growing Deeper...

▶ How long have you followed Jesus?

▶ Have you grown spiritually or are you still in spiritual diapers?

▶ Need a place to start reading in the Bible? Try the "J" books in the New Testament: John, James, and 1, 2 & 3 John.

The Bible to Life

Chapter 18

SDRAM, A Bible Memory Plan

RAM:

Repetition,
Association, and
Meditation.

SDRAM:

Synchronous,
Dynamic,
Repetition,
Association, and
Meditation.

"I will meditate on Your precepts And regard Your ways. I shall delight in Your statutes; *I shall not forget Your word.*" Psalms 119:15-16 (NASB)

Why Should a Follower of Jesus Christ Memorize Bible Verses?

A Christian grows through a **relationship** with Jesus Christ primarily by spending time with Him as they would anyone else that they have a growing and healthy relationship with. This is done through regular and clear communication (communion, community) by talking with God (prayer) and listening to God (reading, studying, and meditating on Scripture). Knowing the Bible is like knowing God's thoughts, intentions and will. But in the everyday business of life, we can't always find the passage of Scripture we need when we want or need it, so practically speaking, memorizing it makes it more readily accessible to us.

Dallas Willard, professor of Philosophy at the University of Southern California, wrote, "Bible memorization is absolutely fundamental to spiritual formation. If I had to choose between all the disciplines of the spiritual life, I would choose Bible memorization, because it is a fundamental way of filling our minds with what it needs. This book of the law shall not depart out of your mouth. That's where you need it! How does it get in your mouth? Memorization."[116]

Chuck Swindoll adds,

I know of no other single practice in the Christian life more rewarding, practically speaking, than memorizing Scripture. . . No other single exercise pays greater spiritual dividends! Your prayer life will be strengthened. Your witnessing will be sharper and much more effective. Your attitudes and outlook will begin to change. Your mind will become alert and observant. Your confidence and assurance will be enhanced. Your faith will be solidified.[117]

---

[116] "Spiritual Formation in Christ for the Whole Life and Whole Person" in Vocatio, Vol. 12, no. 2, Spring, 2001, p. 7.

[117] Growing Strong in the Seasons of Life [Grand Rapids: Zondervan, 1994], p. 61.

Biblical and practical reasons why serious Christians should want to know the word of God and have it in their memory:

A Love for Christ.

Note what Jesus said in Mark 12:30 about us loving our God with all that we are, "and you shall love the Lord your God with all your heart, and with all your soul, and with all your mind, and with all your strength." (NASB) Jesus also taught, "If anyone loves Me, he will keep My word; and My Father will love him, and We will come to him and make Our abode with him. (John 14:23, NASB) Ephesians 6:24 adds, "Grace to all who love our Lord Jesus Christ with an undying love."

A Conformity to Christ.

In 2 Corinthians 3:18b we are informed that believers are "are being transformed into His likeness with ever-increasing glory, which comes from the Lord, Who is the Spirit." Romans 12:2 encourages us to "...not conform any longer to the pattern of this world, but be transformed by the renewing of your mind. Then you will be able to test and approve what God's will is— his good, pleasing and perfect will." Further, Philippians 2:5 reminds us that even our "attitude should be the same as that of Christ Jesus."

A Communion with Christ and the Church.

Colossians 3:16 guides followers of Jesus to "Let the word of Christ dwell in you richly as you teach and admonish one another with all wisdom, and as you sing psalms, hymns and spiritual songs with gratitude in your hearts to God." Hebrews 10:25 adds, "Let us not give up meeting together, as some are in the habit of doing, but let us encourage one another—and all the more as you see the Day approaching.

To Conquer Sin.

In Psalms 119:11 we are told that keeping God's word in our hearts will give us victory over sin! "Your word I have treasured (hidden, kept, saved)[118] in my heart, that I may not sin against you. (NASB) Just two verses earlier the Psalmist asked, "How can a young man keep his way pure? By living according to your word." (Psalms 119:9)

To Defeat Satan.

In the record of Jesus' temptation in the wilderness (Matthew 4:1-11), we find Him using Scripture from memory to defeat Satan every time He is tempted. "It is written..." He said in response to Satan's attempts to lure Him. Such a great example for us to follow! James 4:7 challenges and encourages us to "Submit therefore to God. Resist the devil and he will flee from you." (NASB) Bob Dylan surely got it right years ago when he wrote and sang "You gotta serve somebody, it might be the devil or it might be the Lord, but you gotta serve somebody!" What do you do? Do you submit to and serve God, or do you just let Satan have his way with you?

To Wield the Sword of the Spirit.

We find out about the "sword of the Spirit, which is the word of God" as an integral part of our spiritual armor in Ephesians

---

[118] Hebrew NASB Number: 6845, Hebrew Word: צָפַן, Transliterated Word: tsaphan (860c) Root: a prim. root; to hide, treasure up, keep, save. New American Standard Exhaustive Concordance of the Bible.

6:17. It is the one offensive and defensive weapon mentioned among the articles of armor. With this sword/word, we can fight destructively against the enemy and victoriously for the Kingdom of God! Is your sword at your side? Memorization of Bible passages makes it possible to be ready for battle 24/7!

To Comfort and Counsel People.

Proverbs 25:11 reminds us of the importance of wise and timely words, "A word fitly spoken is like apples of gold in a setting of silver." Pastor John Piper wrote, "When the heart full of God's love can draw on the mind full of God's word, timely blessings flow from the mouth."[119]

To Communicate the Gospel to Unbelievers.

Piper also wrote about the impact of Scripture in our witness for Christ, "Actual verses of the Bible have their own penetrating power. And when they come from our heart, as well as from the Book, the witness is given that they are precious enough to learn."[120] The prophet Isaiah wrote about this penetrating power, "so is My word that goes out from My mouth: It will not return to Me empty, but will accomplish what I desire and achieve the purpose for which I sent it. (Isaiah 55:11)

To Obey God's Commands.

Deuteronomy 6:6-9 states, "These commandments that I give you today are to be upon your hearts. Impress them on your children. Talk about them when you sit at home and when you

---

[119] By John Piper. ©2012 Desiring God Foundation. Website: desiringGod. org.

[120] Ibid.

walk along the road, when you lie down and when you get up. Tie them as symbols on your hands and bind them on your foreheads. Write them on the doorframes of your houses and on your gates."

Deuteronomy 11:18-21 adds, "Fix these words of mine in your hearts and minds; tie them as symbols on your hands and bind them on your foreheads. Teach them to your children, talking about them when you sit at home and when you walk along the road, when you lie down and when you get up. Write them on the doorframes of your houses and on your gates, so that your days and the days of your children may be many in the land that the LORD swore to give your forefathers, as many as the days that the heavens are above the earth."

Joshua 1:7-8 encourages us to "Be strong and very courageous. Be careful to obey all the law my servant Moses gave you; do not turn from it to the right or to the left, that you may be successful wherever you go. Do not let this Book of the Law depart from your mouth; meditate on it day and night, so that you may be careful to do everything written in it. Then you will be prosperous and successful."

John Piper writes, "I'm not into mechanical memorizing. I'm into fighting the fight of faith. I want to memorize Scripture so that I can defeat the devil at 3 o'clock in the afternoon, that's why! It's so that I can minister to a saint in the hospital at 10 o'clock at night if I've forgotten my Bible. This is for our soul. So I carry it around and I review it. Review is so crucial."[121]

---

[121] Ibid.

How Can a Christian Memorize Bible Verses?

Borrowing from the world of computer technology will afford us a memorable acronym for Bible memorization. The term Random Access Memory (RAM) is a form of computer data storage, serving as temporary storage and working space for the operating system and applications.[122] The RAM in a computer functions much like our brains do to our bodies. So, we'll use **RAM** as an acronym for a clear and easy Bible memory system;

Repetition

Like tying our shoes—we have done it so many times we will never forget how to do it. If we choose a passage of Scripture we wish to memorize and say it five times at least twice a day for a week, it is very likely that we will have securely fastened that verse into our memory for a long period of time. Many believers remember the Lord's Prayer because they have said it so many times in church or Sunday school over the years. Remember, everything that is worth anything, costs something. The effort we invest in repeating and reviewing Scripture is an eternal investment!

Remember, everything that is worth anything, costs something!

---

[122] Today, it takes the form of integrated circuits that allow stored data to be accessed in any order with a worst-case performance of constant time. In addition to serving as temporary storage and working space for the operating system and applications, RAM is used in numerous other ways. https://en.wikipedia.org/wiki/Randomaccess_ memory.

Association

It is easy remembering the name of someone with the same name as ours or someone we know very well. So why not associate Bible verses and references with something familiar to us? We can do this by taking a verse we wish to memorize and making some connection with something else that we have a great deal of familiarity with. One example is Matthew 7:11. Here Jesus said, "If you then, being evil, know how to give good gifts to your children, how much more will your Father who is in heaven give what is good to those who ask Him!" This verse can be related to the 7-Eleven convenience store chain. It is a business that is open whenever we need them to provide something "good" or even to pick up a last-minute "gift". We just need to go in and ask (and pay of course). Even though God doesn't give us everything we ask for, Jesus did say He wants to "give us good gifts"!

Another verse that is easy to associate, is John 6:66. Here the apostle John tells about Jesus' "hard teaching" (v. 60) causing some of the large number of disciples to turn away, "From this time many of his disciples turned back and no longer followed him." This number, 666, is also the number for the beast in Revelation 13 (also written by John), whose sole purpose is to turn people away from Christ to worship the antichrist.[123]

Another couple of verses that fit together well with their message is 1 Peter 5:7 and Hebrews 5:7. Notice the reference numbers 5:7 match, and so do the themes of casting anxiety or cares on the Lord. First Peter 5:7 encourages us to "Cast all your anxiety on him because he cares for you." Hebrews 5:7 informs us about our Lord Jesus Christ casting His cares on His Father,

---

[123] Revelation 13:11-18.

"During the days of Jesus' life on earth, he offered up prayers and petitions with loud cries and tears to the one who could save him from death..."

Association is a powerful tool to help with Scripture memorization, so why not come up with some of your own Bible verse associations?

Meditation

Meditation is another excellent means of memorizing God's word. It is defined as "the act or process of meditating."[124] Meditating is in turn defined, "to engage in contemplation or reflection."[125] If we take time to study a passage of Scripture carefully and contemplate on it, we will likely already have most of that passage memorized without any extra effort. We often remember things we like more than we realize, so if we find God's word "sweet" to our "taste" or "sweeter than honey" (Psalms 119:103), we will not have difficulty remembering it. The Psalmist earlier confirmed with this exclaimation in verse 97, "Oh, how I love your law! I meditate on it all day long." The Psalmist not only loved God's law, he noted that his meditation lasted the whole day, which was an acknowledgment that time was another factor to consider in the memorization process. Are you allowing time in your schedule to reflect on Bible verses throughout the day?

---

[124] "1: a discourse intended to express its author's reflections or to guide others in contemplation. 2: the act or process of meditating." https://www.merriam-webster.com/dictionary/meditation.

[125] "1: to engage in contemplation or reflection He meditated long and hard before announcing his decision. 2 : to engage in mental exercise (such as concentration on one's breathing or repetition of a mantra) for the purpose of reaching a heightened level of spiritual awareness." https://www.merriam-webster.com/dictionary/meditate.

Dynamic

Now, let's expand our acronym by adding a letter **D** to the beginning of **RAM** to equal **DRAM.**

DRAM in computer tech is an upgraded type of RAM known as Dynamic Random-Access Memory. It is a type of random-access memory that reaches very high densities.[126] Let's focus on the word "Dynamic". What is it that could make our Scripture memory process dynamic? Prayer. Through prayer and Scripture, we can have a close walk with God and be freed from Satan's deceit and enslavement and empowered to closeness and communion with God. James 4:7-8b says, "Submit therefore to God. Resist the devil and he will flee from you. Draw near to God and He will draw near to you." When we draw near to God, Who is spirit[127], our whole spiritual life is immensely enhanced! With this new enhancement comes a passion to walk in the Spirit[128] and to know and live out the word of God.[129] Are you walking in the Spirit? Could you classify this walk as dynamic?

---

[126] DRAM stores each bit of data in a separate capacitor within an integrated circuit. The advantage of DRAM is its structural simplicity: only one transistor and a capacitor are required per bit, compared to four or six transistors in SRAM. This allows DRAM to reach very high densities. Unlike flash memory, DRAM is volatile memory (cf. non-volatile memory), since it loses its data quickly when power is removed. (Wiki)

[127] "God is spirit, and his worshipers must worship in spirit and in truth." John 4:24.

[128] "If we live by the Spirit, let us also walk by the Spirit." Galatians 5:25 (NASB)

[129] "Take the helmet of salvation and the sword of the Spirit, which is the word of God. Ephesians 6:17

Synchronous

Computer engineers have developed computer memory even further than DRAM to what they now call SDRAM. This is a dynamic random access memory (DRAM) that is synchronized with the system bus and is called Synchronous Dynamic Random Access Memory.[130] Let's take the "S" from synchronizing and apply it to our Bible memory plan, so our expanded acronym becomes **SDRAM.**

One way to synchronize Scripture for the purpose of memorization is adding music to a Bible verse or verses to create memorable songs. There are already many songs written this way that can be learned and sung anywhere, anytime. Songs like Matthew 6:33: "Seek ye first the kingdom of God, and His righteousness, and all these things shall be added unto you, al-le-e-lu, al-lel-u-jah."[131] Other examples which are based on the King James translation, are Micah 6:8; Psalms 100; Hosea 6:3; Ephesians 4:32; Psalms 51:10-12 and many more. Several Christian artists have written songs based on Bible verses and many whole albums are dedicated to scripture memory songs.

There are also several body action songs like "His Banner over me is Love" from Song of Solomon 2:4 and "Cast Your Burden"

---

[130] Classic DRAM has an asynchronous interface, which means that it responds as quickly as possible to changes in control inputs. SDRAM has a synchronous interface, meaning that it waits for a clock signal before responding to control inputs and is therefore synchronized with the computer's system bus. The clock is used to drive an internal finite state machine that pipelines incoming commands. This allows the chip to have a more complex pattern of operation than an asynchronous DRAM, enabling higher speeds.

[131] Amy Grant and Gary Chapman also wrote a contemporary version of this song in the 90's on their album titled, "Songs from the Loft."

from 1 Peter 5:7 (written by the Donut Man) which includes a chorus singing "Higher, higher..." where singers start from a low standing position and reach higher as they sing. The 10 Commandments have actions or hand motions to remember them with and they can be seen at terrenceWsmith.com at the bottom of the home page.

We need to be more proactive in hiding God's word in our hearts. Even if we resort ourselves to singing children's songs and hand motions. The Scriptures are worth remembering at any cost.

RAM:

Repetition,
Association, and
Meditation.

SDRAM:

Synchronous,
Dynamic,
Repetition,
Association, and
Meditation.

Growing Deeper...

▶ Try repeating a Bible verse five times in the morning and again in the evening for a week. At the end quiz yourself and see how well you have done.

▶ Try associating parts of Scripture with something similar and very familiar. Quiz yourself or have someone else quiz you to see how you are doing.

▶ Spend more time than usual on a passage of Scripture that is important to you and ask God to reveal truth to you and speak to you. You will not likely forget the passage anytime soon!

▶ Try writing your own music, actions, symbols, or drawings to Bible verses to make them more memorable and helpful to your walk with Christ. Share them with others to get their feedback so you can adapt and improve them.

The Bible to Life

Chapter 19

SIR, The 3 Wills of God

Sovereign,
Individual, and
Righteous wills of God.

Studying about God's will in the Bible can be very confusing when you first dive in to it. It is really not that complicated but sometimes it is hard to discover what the Bible actually says about it as the discussion is brief and found in several different passages. Theologians solve the dilemma for us by revealing that there are actually three wills of God or three types of His will found in the Bible's pages. It is quite easily remembered with the use of the acronym **SIR**.

Sovereign Will.

The first and generally most obvious type of the will of God in Scripture is the Sovereign will of God. Some scholars call it His determined, directive, or providential will. They, and the passages they reference, note that it is not dependent on us, and we can do nothing to change it. Romans 9 is one of those passages.

> It does not, therefore, depend on man's desire or effort, but on God's mercy. For the Scripture says to Pharaoh: "I raised you up for this very purpose, that I might display my power in you and that my name might be pro-

claimed in all the earth." Therefore God has mercy on whom he wants to have mercy, and he hardens whom he wants to harden. (Romans 9:16-18)

And in the book of Job it says, "God's voice thunders in marvelous ways; he does great things beyond our understanding. He says to the snow, 'Fall on the earth,' and to the rain shower, 'Be a mighty downpour.' So that all men he has made may know his work, he fills all men with fear by His power." (Job 37:5-7) Then hear God's pungent response to Job's defensive speech, "Where were you when I laid the earth's foundation? Tell me, if you understand. Who marked off its dimensions? Surely you know! Who stretched a measuring line across it?" (Job 38:4-5) Some things are only in God's hands.

Individual Will.

Clearly, the Bible teaches God is sovereign over all things and that He has a sovereign will that He may exercise as He chooses. An Individual Will of God is also found in the Bible's pages, which Bible scholars also refer to as His detailed or personal will for each believer in Christ. This Individual Will has to do with His specific plans for us related to His calling on our lives, such as our path of ministry, choice of vocation, and even where we live.

A prime example of this is God's choice of Moses to be His deliver of the people of Israel from the cruel and stubborn Pharaoh of Egypt. In Exodus 3, after revealing Himself to Moses with an inextinguishable fiery bush, He implored, "So now, go. I am sending you to Pharaoh to bring my people the Israelites out of Egypt." (Exodus 3:10, but read the whole chapter) Moses reluctantly agreed to go, but begged God to have someone else or Aaron be the chief speaker and negotiator, which God allowed for a time. Even though we can see God's sovereign will working here, we can also see His individual will for Moses' life being revealed along with his resistance. In fact, God almost took Moses' life on the way to see the Pharoah the first time (Exodus 4:24). God only allowed Moses to excuse himself a few times before Moses realized His joy in being obedient to God's Individual will for him.

Another good example is 75-year-old Abraham. God told him to leave his homeland in Haran (which was a long way from where he was born and raised in Ur) and travel to a far-off country called Canaan which he had never been to before. He responded by faithfully and willingly obeying (Genesis 12). God promised him many descendants, great blessing and that he would be a blessing to many! The passage clearly shows a loving heavenly Father God who asks, guides and commands, but does not coerce, manipulate, or force Abraham into obedience. God had specific plans for Abraham that we get to see unfold in the pages of Scripture.

The Apostle Paul is another perfect example of God's individual will on display. We find Him in Acts 9 being confronted by the resurrected Christ Himself, "He fell to the ground and heard a voice say to him, 'Saul, Saul, why do you persecute me?'

'Who are you, Lord?' Saul asked.

'I am Jesus, whom you are persecuting,' he replied. 'Now get up and go into the city, and you will be told what you must do.'" (Acts 9:4-6)

God's crafted plan for Paul's evangelistic ministry to the Gentiles was revealed to him through Ananias three days later (v. 10-18).

Thank God for the large amount of the written word of God that came by way of this apostle!

An excellent piece of wisdom to keep in mind is that God's will for us is not about us! It is about Him! It is about what He wills and has in store that both benefits His Kingdom, us personally, and those around us! Some people say things like, "I want to know what God's will for **Me** is", when what they should be saying is, "I want to know what **God's** will for me is."

George Mueller had some extremely helpful steps for determining God's individual will:

1. I seek at the beginning to get my heart into such a state that it has no will of its own in regard to a given matter. Nine-tenths of the trouble with people generally is just here. Nine-tenths of the difficulties are overcome when our hearts are ready to do the Lord's will, whatever that may be. When one is truly in this state, it is usually but a little way to the knowledge of what His will is.

2. Having done this, I do not leave the result to feeling or simple impression. If so, I make myself liable to great delusions.

3. I seek the will of the Spirit of God through, or in connection with, the Word of God. The Spirit and the Word must be combined. If I look to the Spirit alone without the Word, I lay myself open to great delusions also. If the Holy Ghost guides us at all, He will do it according to the Scriptures and never contrary to them.

4. Next, I take into account providential circumstances. These often plainly indicate God's will in connection with His Word and Spirit.

5. I ask God in prayer to reveal His will to me aright.

6. Thus, through prayer to God, the study of the Word, and reflection, I come to a deliberate judgment according to the best of my ability and knowledge; and if my mind is thus at peace, and continues so after two or three more petitions, I proceed accordingly. In trivial matters, and in transactions involving the most important issues, I have found this method always effective.[132]

Righteous Will

The final and most common will of God in the Bible is the Righteous Will of God. This is also known as His desired, moral or permissive will. Here, obedience to God's commands, precepts, laws, and statutes is required of believers in order to fulfill it.[133] In the Bible, God is more concerned about who we are than what we do! He is more concerned about character than career.

The key to understanding this will is sanctification and righteousness. Sanctification means to be set apart to God and

God is more concerned about who we are than what we do!

---

[132] Mueller, George, Answers to Prayer. From George Mueller's Narratives. Moody Press, Chicago. p. 6.

[133] For more detail on these words, see chapter 14, The Original GPS.

separated from sin.[134] Righteousness has to do with "doing what is right"[135] and in scripture it always aligns with what God says is right. Jesus informed that His disciples are to "seek first His kingdom and His righteousness, and all these things will be added to you." (Matthew 6:33, NASB)

In regard to sanctification, 1 Thessalonians 4:3 affirms it as God's will for His children:

> For this is the will of God, your sanctification; *that is,* that you abstain from sexual immorality; 4 that each of you know how to possess his own vessel in sanctification and honor, 5 not in lustful passion, like the Gentiles who do not know God; 6 *and* that no man transgress and defraud his brother in the matter because the Lord is *the* avenger in all these things, just as we also told you before and solemnly warned *you.* 7 For God has not called us for the purpose of impurity, but in sanctification. 8 So, he who rejects *this* is not rejecting man but the God who gives His Holy Spirit to you." (1 Thessalonians 4:3-8. NASB)

Since "all our righteous acts are like filthy rags"[136] we must be sanctified by the blood of Christ first in order to be positionally righteous. Then we will be empowered and able to practice

---

[134] Sanctify = "consecration, sanctification." ἁγιασμός (hagiasmos) #38, Root from #37 and #40 ἅγιος (hagios) = "sacred, holy, saints." In Hebrew #6044 qodesh = "dedicated, separated to (God) and from (sin)." NASB and Strong's Concordences.

[135] Righteousness = "righteousness, justice." δικαιοσύνη (dikaiosunê) #1343. NASB Concordance.

[136] "All of us have become like one who is unclean, and all our righteous acts are like filthy rags; we all shrivel up like a leaf, and like the wind our sins sweep us away." (Isaiah 64:6)

righteousness.[137] Hebrews 13:12 reveals this truth, "And so Jesus also suffered outside the city gate to make the people holy through his own blood." The Apostle John adds, "But if we walk in the light, as he is in the light, we have fellowship with one another, and the blood of Jesus, his Son, purifies us from all sin." (1 John 1:7) And in the letter to the Romans, "But God demonstrates his own love for us in this: While we were still sinners, Christ died for us. 9 Since we have now been justified by his blood, how much more shall we be saved from God's wrath through him!" (Romans 5:8-9)

After one is made positionally righteous, then righteousness can be practiced in at least three ways. First, by **obeying God's precepts** from the Bible, which are His rules for righteous living, such as the 10 Commandments. Secondly, by **developing and following principles** which are based on the practical application of biblical precepts to our own lives. Finally, there must be **passion for God and others** by following the Great Commandment to Love God first and others more than ourselves.[138]

---

[137] Theologians discuss two types of righteousness: 1. **Positional** (imputed) righteousness, because of Christ's work on the cross and in glory, and; 2. **Practical** righteousness, through our own obedience to God.

[138] Matthew 22:35-40, "One of them, an expert in the law, tested him with this question: "Teacher, which is the greatest commandment in the Law?" Jesus replied: "'Love the Lord your God with all your heart and with all your soul and with all your mind.' This is the first and greatest commandment. And the second is like it: 'Love your neighbor as yourself.' All the Law and the Prophets hang on these two commandments." Mark 12:28-31 reads, "One of the teachers of the law came and heard them debating. Noticing that Jesus had given them a good answer, he asked him, "Of all the commandments, which is the most important?" "The most important one," answered Jesus, "is this: 'Hear, O Israel, the Lord our God, the Lord is one. Love the Lord your God with all your heart and with all your soul and with all your mind and with all your strength.' The second is this:

The 10 Commandments are a prime example of the moral code for every follower of Christ. In them we find green and red lights regarding behavior. Green for the things we are to do, such as remembering the Sabbath and keeping it holy (the fourth commandment found in Exodus 20:8) and red-light laws pertaining to things we are not to do, such as having other gods (the first command, v. 3). The first four are specifically instructional regarding our relationship with God and the last six specifically concerning our actions towards others.[139]

When thinking of the 10 Commandments, the cross of Jesus Christ comes to mind. The vertical post of the cross compares to the first four commandments, and the horizontal crossbeam to how His followers should treat others. Jesus hung on the cross literally with His arms held wide open to humanity and for humanity! Believers ought to have open arms for those near them as well!

'Love your neighbor as yourself.' There is no commandment greater than these."

[139] Commandments #1 No other gods before God, #2 No idols, #3 Not misusing God's name, and #4 Keeping the Sabbath holy all are part of our relationship with God. Commandments #5 Honoring our parents, #6 Not murdering, #7 not committing adultery, #8 not stealing, #9 not lying and #10 not coveting all have to do with our relationships with other people.

C
o
m
m
a
n
C o m m a n d m e n t s 6-10
m
e
n
t
s
1
-
4

It seems most convincing that the two stone tablets God carved the 10 Commandments on were not evenly distributed with five commandments on each one. Rather, the first stone was more likely for the first four commands relating to God and the second stone contained the last six laws for our relationships with others.

God's laws are given for us to obey and are for our benefit, but we have the freedom to choose what we will do with them. When we obey His commands, we are acting within His righteous will and we will be blessed. When we disobey them, we are not walking in His will and there will be negative consequences to come.

Here are some other scriptures to carefully consider confirming the teaching on God's righteous will:

Ephesians 5:17-21, "So then do not be foolish, *but understand what the will of the Lord is*. And do not get drunk with wine, for that is dissipation, but be filled with the Spirit, speaking to one another in psalms and hymns and spiritual songs, singing and making melody with your heart to the Lord; always giving thanks for all things in the name of our Lord Jesus Christ to God, even the Father; and be subject to one another in the fear of Christ."

1 Thessalonians 4:3-8, "It is God's will that you should be sanctified: that you should avoid sexual immorality; that each of you should learn to control his own body in a way that is holy and honorable, not in passionate lust like the heathen, who do not know God; and that in this matter no one should wrong his brother or take advantage of him. The Lord will punish men for all such sins, as we have already told you and warned you. For God did not call us to be impure, but to live a holy life. Therefore, he who rejects this instruction does not reject man but God, who gives you his Holy Spirit.

1 Thessalonians 5:16-18, "Be joyful always; pray continually; give thanks in all circumstances, for this is God's will for you in Christ Jesus."

1 John 2:15-17, "Do not love the world or anything in the world. If anyone loves the world, the love of the Father is not in him. For everything in the world— the cravings of sinful man, the lust of his eyes and the boasting of what he has and does—comes not from the Father but from the world. The world and its desires pass away, but the man who does the will of God lives forever."

SIR:

Sovereign,
Individual, and
Righteous wills of God.

Wisdom

The Bible does not tell us to ask for God's Individual Will to be revealed to us, but rather to ask for wisdom to make proper decisions as we walk with Him according to His Righteous Will. James 1:5-8 provides further explanation of asking and how to ask (Greek definitions in parenthesis added):

> If any of you lacks wisdom, he should ask God, who gives generously to all without finding fault (denouncing, disgracing, insulting, reviling), and it will be given to him. But when he asks, he must believe (be persuaded, trust, confidence in a truth) and not doubt (judge, waver), because he who doubts is like a wave of the sea, blown and tossed by the wind. That man should not think he will receive anything from the Lord; he is a double-minded (doubting, hesitating) man, unstable in all he does.[140]

Two chapters later, James again writes about wisdom and digs a bit deeper by describing two types of wisdom; earthly and heavenly wisdom and their differences (Greek definitions in parentheses added):

> Who is wise and understanding among you? Let him show it by his good life, by deeds done in the humility that comes from wisdom. But if you harbor bitter envy

---

[140] The definitions in parentheses are from the NASB Concordance.

and selfish ambition in your hearts, do not boast about it or deny the truth. Such "wisdom" does not come down from heaven but is earthly, unspiritual, of the devil (lit. "demonic"). For where you have envy and selfish ambition, there you find disorder (confusion, disturbances) and every evil practice.

But the wisdom that comes from heaven is first of all pure (clean, clear, innocent, modest); then peace-loving (from the root meaning peace, quiet, undisturbed, prosperous), considerate, submissive (impartial, ready to obey), full of mercy and good fruit (harvest, benefits), impartial and sincere (NASB has "without hypocrisy").[141] (James 3:13-17)

Which wisdom do you choose?

The Way of Wisdom Summarized

In a very comprehensive book titled, Decision Making and the Will of God,[142] Dr. Gary Friesen provides a brief summary process for practicing wisdom and walking in God's will. He expertly and succinctly writes the following four guiding steps to walking in wisdom:

1. Where God commands, we must obey.
2. Where there is no command, God gives us freedom (and responsibility) to choose.
3. Where there is no command, God gives us wisdom to choose.

---

[141] Ibid.

[142] Gary Friesen, Decision Making and the Will of God. Multnomah Publishers, Sisters, Oregon, 2004.

4. When we have chosen what is moral and wise, we must trust the sovereign God to work all the details together for good.

Knowing that God is not a perfectionistic tyrant who wishes to see us fail at every turn, but a loving and gracious heavenly Father (see chapter 5) who wants what is best for us and knows what lies ahead of us, makes all the difference in the world in our perspective of life and our ability to walk in grace, peace, and wisdom! Only trust Him now!

Learning to trust that God is sovereign over all things and has control of them, is a major step upward in one's growth and a significant leap forward to peace in one's life!

Growing Deeper...

▶ Are you walking in God's Righteous will for your life?

▶ Are you willing to try Friesen's Way of Wisdom?

▶ Are you willing to trust God the heavenly Father with your life? With your cares?

▶ Pick up a copy of Friesen's book or if you desire to read something quicker, read Just Do Something by Kevin DeYoung.[143] It is much shorter and very direct, with the same biblical focus on God's wisdom in decision making.

---

[143] Kevin DeYoung, Just Do Something. Moody Publishers, Chicago, Illinois, 2009.

The Bible to Life

Chapter 20

Everyone is CALLED

Conviction of God's leading,
Awareness of your gifts and wiring,
Leadership approval,
Lasting desire,
Energy and fulfillment received, and
Done the work already.

Have you ever asked yourself questions like, "Am I meant to do something more with my life? Am I bored, dissatisfied and unhappy with my job or current life status? Do I long for something else—something more fulfilling than what I am doing now?"

If you have been asking these questions, maybe you need to consider a new "calling", or put more commonly, a new vocation. It has been wisely concluded that "if you love your job (calling) you will never work a day in your life."

There is more than one type of calling, especially for Christians. In the Bible we are told that believers are called to salvation, spiritual growth, suffering and service, but most of the time we struggle with the specific service God is calling us to. It is no wonder that it is so difficult for us, since we have so many options, and so many enemies—the world (rebellious mankind),

177

human nature (rebellious selfishness) and spiritual darkness (rebellious evil spirits; Satan and demons).

To make this easier, we must seek God in prayer and studying the Bible, which is His "word" to us. God's word records several characteristics of God's calling that are helpful for us to know to better understand it.

Biblical Characteristics

God's call is obvious. Matthew 4:18-22 recounts the first calling of the disciples by our Lord Jesus, where He approached Peter and Andrew and spoke to them clearly and authoritatively. How do we know this? We know it because of their response—they obeyed Him immediately! When God calls us, it should be unmistakable.

God will call when you are giving your best effort in your present situation. Acts 9 records that this was true with the conversion of Saul, where Jesus called him to apostolic service. We find that Paul was striving to serve God to the best of his ability and power (partly by eliminating what he saw as the Christian cult). Jesus knew Paul's real passion was to please God, so He stopped him on his way to Damascus and confronted him, calling him to preach and suffer for His sake. Paul was busy serving God when Jesus called.

God will call in His time. Certainly, Paul and Ananias were surprised at God's timing when he contacted them. Saul and his companions must have been shocked at Jesus' appearance on the road in front of them in the middle of their trip. Saul lost his sight, and they lost their voices. The timing was so completely unexpected! Ananias questioned the Lord because of Saul's recent persecution of the saints and was probably struggling with his specific call, yet he was obedient. For us, God is full of surprises—He is far above our human condition and level of understanding, "'My thoughts are not your thoughts, neither are your ways my ways,' declares the LORD. 'As the heavens are higher than the earth, so are my ways higher than your ways and my thoughts than your thoughts'" (Isaiah 55:8-9).

God will often call through mature believers. Ananias was informed by the Lord in a vision that Saul would be His "chosen instrument" to carry His name "before the Gentiles and their kings and before the people of Israel" (Acts 9:15). Ananias was God's man to help Paul see with both his eyes and his soul. Proverbs 15:22 reminds us that a person with many counselors is wise and chapter 27:17 says, "As iron sharpens iron, so one man sharpens another." Listen to the godly people around you, like Paul listened to Ananias.

God will call in worship. We find in Acts 13:2 that the Holy Spirit spoke directly to the worshiping believers about Paul and Barnabas' calling: "While they were worshiping the Lord and fasting, *the Holy Spirit said*, 'Set apart for me Barnabas and Saul for the work to which I have *called* them.'" All believers are called *to minister to the Lord* (praise, prayer, offerings, etc.) and should be doing so faithfully, and *to minister for the Lord* (discipling, caring, witnessing). If we are busy serving and worshiping, God will call us there.

If we are busy serving and worshiping, God will call us there.

179

God wants to use your gifts and skills. There are at least twenty-one gifts mentioned in five different passages of Scripture[144] and countless skill sets described throughout it. There must be something in these lists that you and I are to use for God's Kingdom work! Romans 12 (and 1 Corinthians 12-14) teaches that believers are part of a body (v. 5) possessing different gifts for each other's benefit (v. 6; 1 Corinthians 12:11). The Lord also told the Church in Corinth (Corinthians 13) that His gifts are to be motivated by and exercised in love (v. 31) and they are worthless if not so used (vv. 1-4).

Six Keys to Unlock Your Calling

The Bible and Christian experience provide at least six keys to unlock your calling. When you are **CALLED** you will have:

Conviction of God's will to do something. You possess an inner passion, desire and sense of anointing for a task. God may call you personally through: His word (the Bible) as you study it and pray about it; His Spirit as He ministers to yours (remembering that the Holy Spirit's weapon is the Bible, Eph 6:17); instruction from His servants (preachers and teachers); and less commonly,[145] a visit from one of His messengers (angels) and visions and dreams.

Awareness of your wiring. Let's refer to this as the way you think and act. Consider the way God has made you: your gifts (natural and spiritual); talents (abilities and resources); and personality style (the way you interact with others). All of these

---

[144] Romans 12:6-8; 1 Corinthians 12:8-10; 12:28-30; Ephesians 4:11; and Exodus 31:1-5; 35:31-33.

[145] Even in the Bible, visits by angels are extremely rare, as are visions and dreams.

attributes make up who you are and are an important part of the mix in your calling.

Leadership counsel and approval. For example, Christ's call and approval of His disciples in Matthew 4:19-22, and of the Apostle Paul after the resurrection in Acts 9. Or Paul's exhortation to Timothy and future disciples in 2 Timothy 2:2, and church leaders in Ephesians 4:11-13. Further, the Bible uses the terms elder, shepherd and overseer interchangeably, revealing an ordained authority of pastors to teach and lead with the guidance of the Bible and the Holy Spirit.

Lasting desire and commitment to something. If God is at work in your desire to serve Him in a specific way, the passion for it will not soon leave you.

Energy and fulfillment experienced by doing a certain work. You find yourself satisfied and joyful with the tasks you have completed. You come away feeling like your work has had value for the Kingdom of God.

Done the work already. You come to realize that you have been involved in the specific work all along, maybe as a hobby or just for the fun of it. So why not continue what you enjoy doing as an occupation? Don't you really want to "never work another day in your life?" Remember, your job is what you're paid for; your calling is what you're made for!

One note of caution: without leadership approval and counsel, our view of our calling can be entirely self-centered and one-sided! Please remember, God's will for us is not about us! It is about Him—obedience and service are what matters most;

So then do not be foolish, *but understand what the will of the Lord is.* And do not get drunk with wine, for that is dissipation, but be filled with the Spirit, speaking to one another in psalms and hymns and spiritual songs, singing and making melody with your heart to the Lord; always giving thanks for all things in the name of our Lord Jesus Christ to God, even the Father; and be subject to one another in the fear of Christ. (Ephesians 5:17-21)

For this is the will of God, your sanctification... 1 Thessalonians 4:3 (NASB)

God's will for us is not about us! It is about Him.

In everything give thanks; for this is God's will for you in Christ Jesus. 1 Thessalonians 5:18 (NASB)

CALLED:

Conviction of God's leading,
Awareness of your gifts and wiring,
Leadership approval,
Lasting desire,
Energy and fulfillment received, and
Done the work already.

Growing Deeper...

▶ Go back and put yourself in each step of the CALLED acronym and think carefully about how each one applies to you.

▶ What are you called by God to do?

The Bible to Life

Chapter 21

5 Steps to Discovering Your Spiritual GIFTS

Glean from the Scriptures,
Inquire of others,
Feel it out,
Think it through, and
Serve with your gifts.

Have you ever wondered what your spiritual gifts are? Have you considered that you may have more gifts than you are aware of? A useful starting point to discovering your spiritual gifts may be to take a spiritual gifts inventory test. It is a multi-page questionnaire which you can answer and then tabulate the results to find your gifts. The problem with this approach is that it is completely one-sided. It guides you by your opinion and thoughts of yourself, which can be too lofty or too lowly. It would be much more objective to have someone who knows you fill it out with you, but of course, that would take quite a bit of someone's time and still be somewhat subjective. This chapter uses a more well-rounded and probably more accurate approach to discovering your spiritual gifts, summarized and organized by the acronym **GIFTS**:

Glean from the Scriptures. Study the lists of spiritual gifts in the various Biblical passages and gather all the information you can about them. Passages like Romans 12:6-8; 1 Corinthians 12:8-10, 28-30; and Ephesians 4:11 will provide plenty of information. Secondly, examine the function of the gifts in the lives of believers. You will find several examples in Romans chapter 16 and throughout the book of Acts.

Inquire of others. Get the opinion of mature believers you trust to assess and confirm your gifts. Proverbs 15:22 supports this; "Without consultation, plans are frustrated, but with many counselors they succeed." (NASB)

Feel it out. Experiment with your gifts. Try serving with your gifts in your church or mission and see how it goes. Observe whether or not you have found satisfaction and fulfillment while doing so, or if someone you have served has been encouraged in their faith. "From him the whole body, joined and held together by every supporting ligament, grows and builds itself up in love, as each part does its work." (Ephesians 4:16)

Think it through. Reflect, evaluate and pray about all the information you have collected, earnestly asking God to reveal His gifting and calling clearly to you. Ephesians 6:18 instructs us to "pray in the Spirit on all occasions with all kinds of prayers and requests." And finally;

Serve with your gifts. Offer your abilities to the Lord by serving in the area of your giftedness in your local church or mission. First Peter 4:10 confirms that "Each one should use whatever gift he has received to serve others." Paul told Timothy his "son in the faith"[146] the same thing he would tell each of us today, "Do not neglect your gift, which was given you through a prophetic

---

[146] "To Timothy my true son in the faith..." (1 Timothy 1:2)

message when the body of elders laid their hands on you." (1 Timothy 4:14)

With all these suggestions considered together, you should be a short time from finding what your spiritual gifts are. Once you know them, use them! You might be a hand, and my what the body can do with its hands! "Now the body is not made up of one part but of many... Now you are the body of Christ, and each one of you is a part of it." (1 Corinthians 12:14, 27)

GIFTS:

Glean from the Scriptures,
Inquire of others,
Feel it out,
Think it through, and
Serve with your gifts.

Growing Deeper...

▶ What are your gifts?

▶ How are you using them?

▶ What is your part in Christ's church?

The Bible to Life

Chapter 22

Time Management,
A Plan You Can DEPEND On

"If I plan to learn, I must learn to plan."
"If I fail to plan, I plan to fail."

I t seems like every older person you speak to has a common regret—there was never enough time! Especially to accomplish all the important things they wanted to. Time may very well be the most valuable resource we have. So, managing our time wisely is extremely important.

Managing time can enable us to become more productive and efficient. Not just by accomplishing more, but also creating more time for rest, family, church and most of all, personal time with the Lord.

I remember years ago when my children were teenagers. It became apparent to me that they were investing an incredible amount of time playing video games, surfing the net and watching TV and movies.

Time is not recyclable!

One of my sons in particular was investing far too much time in front of a screen. So, I did a little calculating and gave him another perspective on this careless stewardship[147] of precious time. I observed the number of screen hours he accumulated each day to be about 4, and I multiplied them by 356 days a year to get a total of 1424 hours for the year. Then I divided this by 24 hours per day to get 59 days! The equivalent of two months was lost to his life each year to pure entertainment, mainly video games! What was even more eye opening was realizing that every 6 years, a whole year would disappear into the wasteland of electronic entertainment! My son gained a whole new perspective on his use of time and made some wise and appropriate adjustments to his activities. Remember, *time is not recyclable!*

While we all need Sabbath rest, I fear that modern screen time doesn't count for much in that regard. Especially since it did not even exist for millennia and has only been available to us in these seemingly unlimited ways for the last twenty years or so (and TV for several decades before and potentially just as addictive). Of course, there are good and noble ways to use technology, such as the production of this book to help people grow in their relationship with God, and the reproduction of true God-honoring stories on film, Bible teaching podcasts, Bible study websites, etc.

As followers of Jesus Christ, we need to think more about stewarding our time in a God-honoring way. Here are a few steps to managing your time effectively by creating a plan that you can **"DEPEND"** on:

---

[147] "1: the office, duties, and obligations of a steward, 2 : the conducting, supervising, or managing of something especially : the careful and responsible management of something entrusted to one's care stewardship of natural resources." https://www.merriam-webster.com/dictionary/stewardship.

Develop daily time for prayer, study and planning. Do it when you are most aware and clear minded. Proverbs 16:3 says, "Commit to the LORD whatever you do, and your plans will succeed." Our Lord Jesus set the example for us in this since He "...often withdrew to lonely places and prayed." (Luke 5:16)

Establish goals and objectives. Some goals are attainable fairly soon and others must by necessity be set into the future or distant future. Objectives are the specific actions and measurable steps that you need to take to achieve your goal.[148] Proverbs 21:5 promises, "The plans of the diligent lead to profit..." So be diligent at establishing your goals and objectives, and profit from them.

Prioritize tasks & goals. Determine what is most important in your life such as your relationship with God, family, ministry and work (if different from ministry). Don't forget to schedule time for Sabbath rest! This was not only important enough to be listed among the 10 Commandments (Exodus 20), but also necessary for re-charging spiritually, mentally and physically!

Keep in mind that daily and weekly rest are both important. A normal Sabbath is 1 day or 1/7th. of a week, which is a good standard for measuring rest time. Maybe we should use the 1/7th. measurement for daily rest as well. If you sleep 8 hours at night and are left with 16 hours of daytime activity, you could set aside 1/7th. of that time, or 2 hours and 30 minutes for resting time or relaxing or play time.

---

[148] "Goals are the outcomes you intend to achieve, whereas objectives are the specific actions and measurable steps that you need to achieve a goal. Goals and objectives work in tandem to achieve success. If you create goals without clear objectives, you run the risk of not accomplishing your goals." https://www.indeed.com/career- advice/career-development/difference-between-goals-and-objectives.

Proverbs 3:5-6 says, "Trust in the LORD with all your heart and lean not on your own understanding; in all your ways acknowledge Him, and He will make your paths straight."

Employ a scheduler/calendar. Write things down (meetings, appointments, tasks) and determine when they should be done so you will remember later the important things you need to do, as well as other responsibilities. Realistic deadlines help you achieve your goals and result in personal growth and fulfillment. Proverbs 15:23 states, "A man finds joy in giving an apt reply— and how good is a timely word!"

Nab a friend–find an accountability partner. Ask someone to correct you when you err, fail or sin, and advise you when you are uncertain. More wisdom from Proverbs 15:22; "Plans fail for lack of counsel, but with many advisers they succeed." Proverbs 27:17 adds, "As iron sharpens iron, so one man sharpens another."

Determine your course of action, analyze and streamline your schedule. Carefully consider whether or not you are trying to do too much or not enough and adapt your schedule to your priorities. James 4:17 reveals just how important this is; "Anyone, then, who knows the good he ought to do and doesn't do it, sins."

DEPEND:

Develop daily time for prayer, study & planning,
Establish goals and objectives,
Prioritize tasks & goals,
Employ a scheduler/calendar,
Nab a friend, and
Determine your course of action.

Growing Deeper...

▶ Which of the steps above do you need to begin using or start using again? When will you start using them or re-set them?

▶ Pick a time now and commit to managing your time in a way that is fruitful for the Kingdom of God and for glorifying Him and benefiting you!

▶ A life-changing resource worth reading is a book by Christian M.D., Richard A. Swenson called Margin, Restoring Emotional, Physical, and Time Reserves to Overloaded Lives.[149]

---

[149] Margin, Restoring Emotional, Physical, and Time Reserves to Overloaded lives by Richard A. Swenson, (Colorado Springs: NavPress, 2004). Particularly helpful are his prescriptions for restoring emotional energy and time margin.

The Bible to Life

Chapter 23

The DOOR to Eternal Life

Draw them to Jesus,
Open their eyes, and
Open their ears so they will have a
Relationship with Him and receive eternal life!

> So Jesus said to them again, "Truly, truly, I say to you,
> **I am the door** of the sheep. All who came before Me
> are thieves and robbers, but the sheep did not hear
> them. **I am the door**; if anyone enters through Me, he
> will be saved, and will go in and out and find pasture.
> The thief comes only to steal and kill and destroy; I
> came that they may have life, and have it abundantly."
> (John 10:7-10, NASB)

The DOOR

When Jesus describes Himself as a **door** for the sheep in this
passage, He is reinforcing the point that He is "the way and the
truth and the life" as stated precisely a few chapters later (in
John 14:6[150]). This figure of speech was universally understood
in Palestine at the time, referring to the door or gate to a corral
or pen for the sheep to stay in at night:

---

[150] John 14:6; "Jesus answered, 'I am the way and the truth and the life. No
one comes to the Father except through me.'"

During the cool winter months, sheep were kept inside a pen at night; the pen usually had a stone wall, which might have briers on top of it (winter was approaching at the time of this feast)... Sheep were led "in" and "out" (Numbers 27:17; 2 Samuel 5:2) of the sheepfold to and from pasture. Several scholars have cited a modern example of shepherds sleeping across the gateway to serve both as shepherd and door.[151]

Unmistakably, the sheep are the followers of Jesus and He is their point of entry into the Kingdom and their reliable protector and provider. He is the one who saves them, protects them, and provides pasture for them. The pasture was food and sustenance for the livestock. What more does one need than that? Protection from all harm and freedom to go in and out where there is food and comfort!

We should be experiencing life exceedingly abundantly above other things as Jesus' sheep!

Additionally, Jesus encouraged that His followers would "have life and have it abundantly." The word abundantly is also translated, "exceedingly, beyond measure, exceedingly abundantly above."[152] We should be experiencing life exceedingly abundantly above other things as Jesus' sheep!

Now, since Jesus is this amazing **DOOR**, let us pray for those who are not yet His sheep, that God our heavenly Father will

---

[151] The IVP Bible Background Commentary, New Testament.

[152] Abundantly = beyond measure, vehemently, more abundantly, very highly, exceeding abundantly above, exceeding. περισσός, Transliteration: perissos, Phonetic Pronunciation: per-is-sos'. 4053. Root: from <G4012> (peri) (in the sense of beyond). Strong's Dictionary.

Draw them to Jesus, Open their eyes and Open their ears so they will have a Relationship with Him and receive eternal life!

Draw them to Jesus.

The Apostle John wrote that Jesus said, "No one can come to me unless the Father who sent me **draws** him, and I will raise him up at the last day." (John 6:44) A few chapters later, "Jesus answered, "I am the way and the truth and the life. No one comes to the Father except through me." (John 14:6) God draws people to Jesus and Jesus is the only way to God and Heaven. Pray for those who have not yet been drawn to Jesus!

So, they can Open their Eyes.

"The god of this age has **blinded** the minds of unbelievers, so that they **cannot see** the light of the gospel of the glory of Christ, who is the image of God. For we do not preach ourselves, but Jesus Christ as Lord, and ourselves as your servants for Jesus' sake. For God, who said, 'Let light shine out of darkness,' made his light shine in our hearts to give us the light of the knowledge of the glory of God in the face of Christ." (2 Corinthians 4:4-6)

The Apostle Paul gave his personal testimony of coming to Christ and his own calling to "open their eyes".

> On one of these journeys I was going to Damascus with the authority and commission of the chief priests. About noon, O king, as I was on the road, **I saw a light** from heaven, brighter than the sun, blazing around me and my companions. We all fell to the ground, and I heard a voice saying to me in Aramaic, "Saul, Saul, why do you persecute me? It is hard for you to kick against the goads."

Then I asked, "Who are you, Lord?"

"I am Jesus, whom you are persecuting," the Lord replied. "Now get up and stand on your feet. I have appeared to you to appoint you as a servant and as a witness of what you have seen of me and what I will show you. I will rescue you from your own people and from the Gentiles. I am sending you to them to **open their eyes** and turn them from darkness to light, and from the power of Satan to God, so that they may receive forgiveness of sins and a place among those who are sanctified by faith in me." (Acts 26:12-18)

God is also wanting us to open the eyes of lost people near us. Do you remember Jesus' command to "Go and make disciples" and to be "teaching them to obey everything I have commanded you..."?

I remember a time when my kids were very young, and my second son Matt was about four years old. We were on a beach in sunny South Carolina, and we were looking at something in the ocean that was curiously just out of sight. Noting that someone down the beach had binoculars, my son joyfully exclaimed a solution, "Let's borrow those guy's barnacles!"

Even though Matt was mistaken about what to call the binoculars, he observed a solution to clearly seeing something out of normal sight range and was willing to do what was needed to see it. What are you doing to help blind eyes see Jesus? Are you willing to borrow someone's "barnacles"?

and **Open their Ears.**

Jesus once proclaimed from His Scriptures, the Old Testament, the need for people to have their ears opened, "It is written in the Prophets: 'They will all be taught by God.' Everyone who **listens** to the Father and learns from him comes to me." (John 6:45) If people will listen to God they will have the opportunity to find Jesus! But how will they be enabled to listen to Him? Romans 10:14-15 answers with a question; "How, then, can they call on the one they have not believed in? And how can they believe in the one of whom they have not heard? And how can they **hear** without someone preaching to them? And how can they preach unless they are sent? As it is written, 'How beautiful are the feet of those who bring **good news!**'"

The Good News comes by way of preaching, and the good news about the Good News for those who are not officially pastors and preachers, is that preaching in the Bible is connected to the Gospel not the pulpit. In other words, while preaching may be done from the pulpit, it may be done by anyone as it originates with heralding the Good News of Jesus' atonement (death on the cross to pay for our sins entirely) by all disciples of Jesus Christ, including you and me! Everywhere in the New Testament where the word for preaching is used, it is connected with the proclamation of the Gospel, not the teaching of God's word.[153] You are meant to be a preacher too!

You are meant to be a preacher too!

---

[153] kēryssō [κηρύσσω] is a verb meaning "preach." <G2784> The underlying sense is that of making proclamation after the manner of a herald. kēryssō is found in approximately sixty contexts. Kērygma [κήρυγμα], <G2782> is a noun derived from kēryssō, meaning "preaching" in all eight occurrences of the term. Kērygma refers to the content of the proclamation of God's word in the Old Testament and the gospel of Christ in the New. Strong's

On another occasion, Jesus informed His disciples that the Holy Spirit would also speak to people about Him, "When the Counselor comes, whom I will send to you from the Father, the Spirit of truth who goes out from the Father, he will **testify about me.**" (John 15:26) We must never forget we have an especially influential and powerful partner in the Holy Spirit with our preaching that will open many ears to the Gospel!

So they can have a **Relationship with Him.**

"Now this is eternal life: that they may **know you,** the only true God, and Jesus Christ, whom you have sent." (John 17:3) Notice in His prayer that Jesus described eternal life as a relationship, not a reward. Knowing God the Father and God the Son are what eternal life is about. It is a relationship that is eternal, and all life comes from and is sustained by God!

"Jesus described eternal life as a relationship, not a reward."

Jesus reinforced the importance of a relationship with Him when describing coming judgment and those He would reject, even after they performed great works for Him:

Not everyone who says to me, "Lord, Lord," will enter the kingdom of heaven, but only he who does the will of my Father who is in heaven.

Dictionary. kēryssō describes the preaching ministry of John the Baptist (Matt. 3:1; Mark 1:4 ff.; Luke 3:3; Acts 10:37); Jesus' preaching activity (Matt. 4:17, 23; 11:1; Mark 1:14, 39; Luke 4:18 ff.; 8:1); and the apostolic proclamation of the gospel (Matt. 10:7; Mark 3:14; Luke 9:2; Acts 8:5; 19:13; 20:25). The usage of kēryssō indicates that Christ is the focus of New Testament preaching (cf. 1 Cor. 1:23; 15:12; 2 Cor. 1:19; 4:5; 11:4; Phil. 1:15; 1 Tim. 3:16). Expository Dictionary of Bible Words.

Many will say to me on that day, "Lord, Lord, did we not prophesy in your name, and in your name drive out demons and perform many miracles?" Then I will tell them plainly, "I never **knew you**. Away from me, you evildoers!" (Matthew 7:21-23)

It is clear that we must know God and that our works won't save us, but it is also obvious that Jesus wants us to obey Him. The Apostle John agreed:

We know that we have come to **know him** if we obey his commands. The man who says, "I **know him**," but does not do what he commands is a liar, and the truth is not in him. But if anyone obeys his word, God's love is truly made complete in him. This is how we **know** we are in him: Whoever claims to live in him must walk as Jesus did." (1 John 2:3-6)

A few chapters later he adds, "We know also that the Son of God has come and has given us understanding, so that we may **know him** who is true. And we are in him who is true—even in his Son Jesus Christ. He is the true God and eternal life." (1 John 5:20)

How is your relationship with Jesus?

The **DOOR**:

Draw them to Jesus,
Open their eyes, and
Open their ears so they will have a
Relationship with Him and receive eternal life!

Growing Deeper...

▶ When is the last time you prayed for someone to be drawn to Jesus?

▶ Do you have a list of people you think need the DOOR? Will you open it by making a list and commit to praying for them?

The Bible to Life

Chapter 24

CARE to Share

Compassionate,
Alert, and
Ready to
Evangelize.

Sharing our faith in Jesus Christ is often difficult, but why is it? Why are we afraid to reveal the most important and life-changing relationship we have ever had with others around us? Is it because we are afraid to hurt someone's feelings or lose their friendship? Are we embarrassed? Do we think we do not have the right personality to be so forward with our beliefs? Are we afraid of the culture that is increasingly opposing Bible believing Christians?

Whatever the problem is, we have been given a mandate by our Lord Jesus to "Go into all the world and preach the good news to all creation..." (Mark 16:15) and to "...make disciples of all nations..." (Matthew 29:19). So how will we bring ourselves to accomplish this task? Let me suggest four simple and powerful steps embodied in the acronym **CARE** that should help. We must be Compassionate, Alert and Ready to Evangelize!

Compassionate.

I had just graduated from Bible college and had no ministry opportunity to serve in, so I worked heavy equipment construction with my older brother. Since the time that I was 14 years of age, I had a passion to serve Christ, yet I had developed little compassion for people. This reality hit me very hard one day about nine years later when I was working a construction job.

We had a contract to remove old fuel tanks from a small hospital and needed temporary workers. One of them was a young man just 18 years of age, who didn't listen very well and didn't normally show up to work on time. I was assisting my brother as a foreman for the job and I didn't have much patience with him. I knew he didn't know Jesus and I knew I should share my faith with him, but I was very impatient and focused on doing the work well and on time. If anything, I probably pushed him away from faith.

One day, he didn't show up for work, and we inquired of his family as to why. The shocking response was that earlier that morning he'd been found dead in his room hanging from a self-made noose! I was ridden with guilt over his death, since I had spent more time with him than anyone else on the job site, and I had not felt or expressed any compassion for him and his situation. If only I had invested more time getting to know him, I probably would have discovered how desperate he was for love and friendship and shared with him his biggest need—Jesus Christ. Since that event, I've tried to always be aware of where people are at spiritually around me and be prepared to share my faith in Christ with them.

Unlike me, Jesus was compassionate. Note how He was "deeply moved" and wept along with Mary and her companions over Lazarus and his passing.

> When Jesus saw her weeping, and the Jews who had come along with her also weeping, he was deeply moved in spirit and troubled.
>
> "Where have you laid him?" he asked. "Come and see, Lord," they replied.
>
> Jesus wept.
>
> Then the Jews said, "See how he loved him!" (John 11:33-36)

Jesus also prayed with passion for His disciples in the Garden of Gethsemane the night before He was betrayed.

> My prayer is not for them alone. I pray also for those who will believe in me through their message, that all of them may be one, Father, just as you are in me and I am in you. May they also be in us so that the world may believe that you have sent me. I have given them the glory that you gave me, that they may be one as we are one: I in them and you in me. May they be brought to complete unity to let the world know that you sent me and have loved them even as you have loved me.
>
> Father, I want those you have given me to be with me where I am, and to see my glory, the glory you have given me because you loved me before the creation of the world.

Righteous Father, though the world does not know you, I know you, and they know that you have sent me. I have made you known to them, and will continue to make you known in order that the love you have for me may be in them and that I myself may be in them. (John 17:20-26).

Jesus Himself often prayed with tears.

Jesus Himself often prayed with tears: "During the days of Jesus' life on earth, he offered up prayers and petitions with loud cries and tears to the one who could save him from death, and he was heard because of his reverent submission." (Hebrews 5:7) In turn, the Apostle Paul encouraged believers to be tender-hearted towards others; "Be kind to one another, tender-hearted, forgiving each other, just as God in Christ also has forgiven you." (Ephesians 4:32, NASB).

Alert.

We must always be watchful for when others are inquisitive of or ready to receive the Gospel and share our faith in Christ as our Savior and Lord. We should also be constantly aware of the enemy's attempts to interfere. Consider these verses:

"And pray in the Spirit on all occasions with all kinds of prayers and requests. With this in mind, **be alert** and always keep on praying for all the saints." (Ephesians 6:18)

"So then, let us not be like others, who are asleep, but let us **be alert** and self-controlled." (1 Thessalonians 5:6)

"Be self-controlled and **alert**. Your enemy the devil prowls around like a roaring lion looking for someone to devour." (1 Peter 5:8)

and

Ready.

We need to be prepped and available to take the Good News to others in need of the gospel at any time; "...and with your feet fitted with the **readiness** that comes from the gospel of peace." (Ephesians 6:15). The Apostle Peter challenged Christ followers similarly; "But in your hearts set apart Christ as Lord. Always **be prepared** to give an answer to everyone who asks you to give the reason for the hope that you have. But do this with gentleness and respect." (1 Peter 3:15).

to

Evangelize with the Gospel of Jesus Christ.

The term "evangelism" comes from a transliteration[154] of the Greek New Testament word euanggelion, which is a combination of the words "good" and "message" or "news" (from anggelos meaning "angel, messenger") and translates as "good news" and "gospel".[155] It is the good news that Jesus Christ came to

---

[154] The definition of transliteration is "to represent or spell in the characters of another alphabet." See https://www.merriam-webster.com/dictionary/transliteration.

[155] εὐαγγέλιον #2098, The root is from the same as 2097; εὐαγγελίζω (euaggelizô), "to announce good news". Root from 2095 and 32a; 2095 εὖ (eu) = "well, good" and 32a ἄγγελος (anggelos) = "a messenger, angel". List of English Words and Number of Times Used: good news (1), gospel (73), gospel's (2). NASB Concordance.

earth and died as a ransom[156] (see Mk. 10:45)[157] for our sin (paying a debt we could never pay) and rose from the dead, proving that all who "know" Him (Mt. 7:21-23)[158] will one day be resurrected as well to eternal life. (1 Cor. 15:20-22)[159]

Common Questions About Evangelism

How a person can know if they or someone else they know is truly a Christ follower, a real Christian?

The Apostle John in 1 John 2:3-6 gives the following direct practical answer:

> We know that we have come to know him if we obey his commands. The man who says, "I know him," but does not do what he commands is a liar, and the truth is not in him. But if anyone obeys his word, God's love is truly made complete in him. This is how we know we

[156] "Redemption price, acquittal", #487, ἀντίλυτρον,(antilytron). Strong's Talking Greek & Hebrew Dictionary.

[157] Mk 10:45 "For even the Son of Man did not come to be served, but to serve, and to give his life as a ransom for many." 1 Timothy 2:6 "who gave himself as a ransom for all men—the testimony given in its proper time." Ephesians 1:7 "In him we have redemption through his blood, the forgiveness of sins, in accordance with the riches of God's grace.

[158] Mt 7:21-23 "Not everyone who says to me, 'Lord, Lord,' will enter the kingdom of heaven, but only he who does the will of my Father who is in heaven. 22 Many will say to me on that day, 'Lord, Lord, did we not prophesy in your name, and in your name drive out demons and perform many miracles?' 23 Then I will tell them plainly, 'I never knew you. Away from me, you evildoers!'"

[159] 1 Cor 15:20-22 "But Christ has indeed been raised from the dead, the firstfruits of those who have fallen asleep. 21 For since death came through a man, the resurrection of the dead comes also through a man. 22 For as in Adam all die, so in Christ all will be made alive."

are in him: Whoever claims to live in him must walk as Jesus did.

Why do we need to define what a Christian is?

According to George Barna and the Cultural Research Center at Arizona Christian University, in the American Worldview Inventory,[160] the views on what it means to be a Christian are changing quickly and have become increasingly diverse.

Just Have Faith

The context for the changing views on faith in America is exemplified by the fact that almost *two out of every three adults (63%) say that having some type of religious faith is more important than which faith a person aligns with.*

Shockingly, *a large majority of people who describe themselves as Christians (68%) embrace that idea,* including those who attend *evangelical (56%)* and *Pentecostal (62%)* churches, even though such thinking conflicts with the teaching typical of such churches. Even higher percentages of people attending *mainline Protestant (67%)* and *Catholic (77%)* churches believe that having some type of religious faith matters more than one's choice of faith. Six out of ten people who are aligned with non-Christians faiths (61%) reflected that same sentiment.

---

[160] American Worldview Inventory 2020 – FULL Release #8: Views of Sin and Salvation. https://www.arizonachristian.edu/culturalresearchcenter/research/

The Bible to Life

The Irrelevance of Sin

Concern about personal sin is on the wane in the United States. Even though seven out of ten adults claim to be Christian, and another one out of ten adults belongs to some other faith group that discourages sinful behavior, *only slightly more than half of U.S. adults (56%) say they consciously and consistently attempt to avoid sinning because they know it offends God.*

The lack of concern about breaking God's laws is further witnessed by the finding that a plurality of adults *(48%) believes that if a person is generally good, or does enough good things during their life, they will "earn" a place in Heaven.* Only one-third of adults (35%) disagree with that notion.

Amazingly, a majority of people who describe themselves as Christian (52%) accept a works-oriented means to God's acceptance. Even more shocking, however, is that huge proportions of people associated with churches whose official doctrine says eternal salvation comes only from embracing Jesus Christ as savior, and not from being or doing good, believe that a person can qualify for Heaven by being or doing good.[161]

Why do Christians or followers of Christ evangelize?

Christian disciples are commissioned to be messengers of the good news. At the time of Christ's ascension to Heaven, Mt. 28:18-20 records "The Great Commission" that Jesus required of them:

---

[161] Ibid.

Then Jesus came to them and said, 'All authority in heaven and on earth has been given to me. Therefore go and make disciples of all nations, baptizing them in the name of the Father and of the Son and of the Holy Spirit, and teaching them to obey everything I have commanded you. And surely I am with you always, to the very end of the age.

Note the five verbs in this Great Commission:

1. "Go" which means to "go, depart, proceed" or "as you go, having gone".[162]

2. "Make" disciples is translated "to be a disciple, to make a disciple" (pupil or learner).[163]

3. "Baptize" is defined as "to immerse, fully emerge, sink, dip"[164] or "to identify with the cause of Christ, His person and work."[165]

4. "Teach" means "to teach, instruct."[166]

---

[162] Go = "depart, proceed" or "as you go, having gone."Aorist participle, 4198, πορεύομαι, *(poreuomai)*, Root: from ochtheô *poros*. NASB Concordance.

[163] Make disciples = "to be a disciple, to make a disciple" (pupil or learner), 3100, μαθητεύω,(mathêteuô), Root: from 3101 "disciple, pupil", root from 3129 "to learn". NASB Concordance.

[164] Baptize = "to immerse, fully emerge, sink, dip, wash". 907, βαπτίζω. (baptizô), Root: from 911; List of English Words and Number of Times Used: Baptist (3), baptize (9), baptized (51), baptizes (1), baptizing (10), ceremonially washed (1), undergo (1). NASB and Strong's and Thayer's Concordances.

[165] The Sonlife Strategy, Dann Spader. P. 13.

[166] Teach = "to teach, instruct."1321, διδάσκω, (didaskô), Root: a redupl. caus. form of Διός daô (to learn); NASB Concordance.

5. "Preach" is translated "to be a herald, proclaim."[167]

Mark 16:15-20 provides us with more information about this directive for His disciples:

> He said to them, "Go into all the world and preach the good news to all creation. Whoever believes and is baptized will be saved, but whoever does not believe will be condemned. And these signs will accompany those who believe: In my name they will drive out demons; they will speak in new tongues; they will pick up snakes with their hands; and when they drink deadly poison, it will not hurt them at all; they will place their hands on sick people, and they will get well."
>
> After the Lord Jesus had spoken to them, he was taken up into heaven and he sat at the right hand of God. Then the disciples went out and preached everywhere, and the Lord worked with them and confirmed his word by the signs that accompanied it.

Why is the Good News so important?

Here are five Biblical reasons the Good News is so vital:

1. People are born in sin and are already separated from God by it. Romans 3:23 states, "... for all have sinned and fall short of the glory of God."

2. People are lost and need of a savior. Luke 19:10 quotes Jesus saying, "For the Son of Man came to seek and to save the lost."

---

[167] Preach = "to be a herald, proclaim", κηρύσσω, (kêrussô), 2784. Ibid.

3. People deserve punishment for sin and the end result is the Lake of Fire, which we should not want anyone to end up in, "If anyone's name was not found written in the book of life, he was thrown into the lake of fire." (Revelation 20:15)[168]

4. Sinners need a new start, and Christ alone can make them new. Second Corinthians 5:17 teaches this, "Therefore, if anyone is in Christ, he is a new creation; the old has gone, the new has come!"

5. People were designed to worship and serve the Creator. Ephesians 2:10 reveals, "For we are God's workmanship, created in Christ Jesus to do good works, which God prepared in advance for us to do."

How are People Coming to Christ?

Church Growth expert Gary L. McIntosh surveyed over one thousand people in forty-three states and shares the following remarkable results of how people are coming to Jesus Christ today, revealing the powerful influence of family and friends on the lost:[169]

---

[168] Revelation 20:11-15 "Then I saw a great white throne and him who was seated on it. Earth and sky fled from his presence, and there was no place for them. And I saw the dead, great and small, standing before the throne, and books were opened. Another book was opened, which is the book of life. The dead were judged according to what they had done as recorded in the books. The sea gave up the dead that were in it, and death and Hades gave up the dead that were in them, and each person was judged according to what he had done. Then death and Hades were thrown into the lake of fire. The lake of fire is the second death. If anyone's name was not found written in the book of life, he was thrown into the lake of fire."

[169] How Are People Actually Coming to Faith Today? By Gary L. McIntosh, http://magazine.biola.edu/article/16-

> Family Member: 43.2%
> Staff Member: 17.3%
> Friend: 15.7%
> Other: 10.9%
> Lay Teacher: 8.3%
> Neighbor: 2.9%
> Work Colleague: 1.8%

What Keeps People from Coming to Christ?

There are several answers to this question and the most common one in the past besides church goers simply not engaging in evangelism, was hypocrisy among Christians and churches. In a more recent Pew Research survey, it was revealed that the tide had changed a bit. It recorded that people said they had other ways to practice faith:

> Overall, the single most common answer cited for not attending religious services is "I practice my faith in other ways," which is offered as a very important reason by 37% of people who rarely or never attend religious services.[170]

An equal number of people shared their dissatisfaction with what they saw or perceived about church:

> A similar share mention things they dislike about religious services or particular congregations, including one-in-four who say they have not yet found a house of worship they like, one-in-five who say they dislike the

---

fall/how-are-people-actually-coming-to-faith-today/ Gary surveyed over one thousand people in forty-three states.

[170] https://www.pewresearch.org/religion/2018/08/01/why-americans-go-to-religious-services/.

sermons, and 14% who say they do not feel welcome at religious services.[171]

Sometimes when it comes to sharing our faith, it may be more important to be like Jesus than to merely talk about Him. Better to walk than talk, or better to walk in Christ's light than the spotlight! It is believed that St. Francis of Assisi (founder of the Franciscan Order, c. 1182–October 3 1226) said, "Preach Jesus, and if necessary, use words."[172] But what can be confirmed that he actually wrote about this was, "All the Friars… should preach by their deeds."[173] D.L. Moody once expressed similar wisdom, "Out of 100 men, one will read the Bible, the other 99 will read the Christian."[174]

Romans 10:14 makes it clear however, that Christlikeness must be paired with preaching; "How, then, can they call on the one they have not believed in? And how can they believe in the one of whom they have not heard? And **how can they hear without someone preaching to them?**"

It is better to walk in Christ's light than the spotlight!

---

[171] Ibid.

[172] *The Strong Family* (1991) by Chuck Swindoll, p.9 (Insight For Living).

[173] https://www.baptistpress.com/resource-library/news/first-person-that-famous-quote-from-st-francis-he-never-said-it/ and https://en.wikiquote.org/wiki/Francis_of_Assisi.

[174] https://www.azquotes.com/author/10304-Dwight_L_Moody/tag/inspiring.

Preparation is also very important as 1 Peter 3:15 challenges, "But in your hearts set apart Christ as Lord. Always be **prepared to give an answer** to everyone who asks you to give the reason for the hope that you have. But do this with gentleness and respect."

According to professor and author Michael Green, the effect of our Witness may be weighed on a balance between our Walk and our Words:[175] The way we act and behave in front of those who know us well normally says more about the gospel than we can successfully articulate. Oppositely, with new acquaintances we usually have only words and thoughts available to share Christ with them.

<u>Walk</u>   <u>Words</u>

(Godly Character/   (Preaching/
Christ-like living)   Respectful conversation)

What is a true Biblical Christian testimony and how do we share it?

The Apostle Paul wrote to Timothy his "son in the faith" (v. 2), who was the pastor of the church in Ephesus at the time, about what a good testimony looks like:

> I thank Christ Jesus our Lord, who has given me strength, that he considered me faithful, appointing me to his service. Even though I was once a blasphemer and a persecutor and a violent man, I was shown mercy because I acted in ignorance and unbelief. The grace of

---

[175] Class lecture notes from Evangelism class at Moody Theological Seminary referencing Dr. Michael Green's Witness illustration.

our Lord was poured out on me abundantly, along with
the faith and love that are in Christ Jesus.

Here is a trustworthy saying that deserves full acceptance: Christ Jesus came into the world to save sinners—of whom I am the worst. But for that very reason
I was shown mercy so that in me, the worst of sinners,
Christ Jesus might display his unlimited patience as
an example for those who would believe on him and
receive eternal life. Now to the King eternal, immortal,
invisible, the only God, be honor and glory for ever
and ever. Amen. (1 Timothy 1:12-17)

Paul offers three parts to a Biblical Christian testimony in his
opening remarks of his letter:

1. **What he was before Jesus Christ:** A blasphemer, violent
    persecutor, worst of sinners, ignorant, and unbelieving
    (v. 13, 15, 16).

2. **What Christ did for him:** He was shown mercy, grace
    poured out abundantly, along with faith and love,
    received unlimited patience, and was given eternal life
    (v. 13, 14, 16).

3. **Who he is now in Christ:** A faithful servant, possessing
    eternal life (v. 12).

So, let's personalize these three points to our conversion story
and remember it this way:

1. What **I was** before Jesus Christ.

2. What **Christ** did for **me**.

3. Who **I am now** in Christ.

This is a powerful testimony, giving glory to God and sharing the truth about a biblical conversion!

In a session with the Lausanne International Conference on Evangelism, the late Dr. John Stott agreed and declared the responsibility of preaching the gospel message to be more important than being present when a decision is made for Christ; "We are commanded to share it, not harvest it."[176] He further stated that the gospel must be defined by the message, not the methods.

How Did Jesus Evangelize?

In John chapter 3, in the "Nic at Night" passage (when Nicodemus came to see Jesus at night), we find at least 12 things Jesus did to guide Nic to believe in Him:

1. Jesus made Himself available to Nicodemus (v. 2).
2. He was unconcerned with cultural boundaries (v. 1-3).
3. He listened to Nic and answered his questions (v. 4-5).
4. He understood Nic and knew what was on his mind (v. 3).
5. He hooked Nic with a statement that begged a response (v.

---

[176] Published version of John Stott's plenary address given at the First International Congress on World Evangelization in Lausanne, Switzerland in 1974. https://www.lausanne.org/content/john-stott-biblical-basis-of-evangelism. In his travels around the world, Billy Graham met many leaders who were disconnected from each other. He felt called to bring these leaders together, thus beginning a movement of connections marked by a spirit of humility, friendship, prayer, study, partnership, and hope, which Graham called 'the spirit of Lausanne'. It is in this spirit that world congresses, global gatherings, and issue-specific forums and consultations have been convened for over 40 years, resulting in numerous connections, initiatives, and resources.

6. He taught Nic biblical and spiritual truth (v. 5-21).
7. He used illustrations to clarify His teaching (v. 8, 19-20).
8. He built on Nic's existing faith (v. 10).
9. He confronted Nic regarding his need (v. 10).
10. He established common ground, common beliefs (v. 14).
11. He moved straight to the heart of the Gospel (summarizing His message, v. 16-21 to believe, v. 16 & 18 to belong, and v. 20-21 to behave).
12. He revealed the Son of God to Nic (v. 16-21).

In John Chapter 4, with the woman at the well, Jesus employed almost identical tactics and teaching as He did with Nic:

1. Jesus initiated the conversation by asking a question of the woman (v. 7).
2. He was unconcerned with cultural boundaries (v. 9).
3. He listened to the woman and answered her questions (v. 10, 13-14).
4. Jesus understood her and knew what was on her mind (v. 12-13).
5. He hooked her with a statement that begged a response (v. 10).
6. He taught her biblical and spiritual truth (v. 21-24).
7. He used illustrations to clarify His teaching (v. 13-14).
8. He built on her existing faith (v. 12-13, 19-21).
9. He confronted her regarding her need (v. 16-18).
10. He established common ground, common beliefs (v. 13-14).
11. He moved straight to the heart of the Gospel, summarizing His message (v. 13-14, 21-24, God is Spirit, man needs Spiritual water).
12. He revealed Himself to her (v. 26).

Notice that Jesus initiated the conversation in each of the above cases and then listened carefully to each person's responses. Knowing them well, and building on their existing faith, His next words continued to present related truth that focused more closely on the gospel message. He wisely utilized interesting and understandable illustrations to clarify His good news. Does this sound complicated? Can you do this too? Jesus exemplified a simple and straight forward method for sharing faith in Him with others that anyone can follow!

Jesus exemplified a simple and straight forward method for sharing faith.

CARE:

Compassionate,
Alert, and
Ready to
Evangelize.

Growing Deeper...

▶ What is the temperature of your CARE thermometer?

▶ Are you all set to share your faith in Christ right now? Are you Alert and Ready?

▶ Do you have a plan to Evangelize your lost family and friends? What is it?

▶ The best place to start is prayer. Do you pray for unsaved family, friends and neighbors? Will you start now?

Suggested Books on Evangelism:

Living Proof, Sharing the Gospel Naturally, by Jim Peterson

Lifestyle Evangelism, Crossing Traditional Boundaries to Reach the Unbelieving World, Joseph C. Aldrich

Tell Someone: You Can Share the Good News, by Greg Laurie

Out of the Salt Shaker, by Rebecca Manley Pippert

Master Plan of Evangelism, by Robert E. Coleman

How to Bring Them to Christ, by R.A. Torrey

Share Jesus Without Fear, by William Faye and Ralph Hodge

Introducing World Missions, a Biblical, Historical, and Practical Survey by A. Scott Moreau Gary R. Corwin, and Gary B. McGee

Anthropological Insights for Missionaries, by Paul G. Hiebert

Breaking Down Walls, A Model for Reconciliation in an Age of Racial Strife, by Raleigh Washington and Glen Kehren

Conclusion

Thank you for reading! It is my prayer that these 24 chapters of acronyms and acrostics help you remember God's Word better, and cause you to grow closer to the heavenly Father as a result! They have certainly helped me in my walk with Him and drastically improved my memory when teaching about Him and the Bible. They have also often reminded me of how good and holy God is and what He wants for me and how to serve Him better. I can only hope and pray the same will be true for you as well!

For more information and for future memory aiding articles, please visit **theBibletoLife.com** or the companion website **terrenceWsmith.com**. There you will find some of the chapters already published on the sites, with more articles to come. You will also be able to request the articles as PDF's or printed pamphlets.

"And now, dear children, continue in him, so that when he appears we may be confident and unashamed before him at his coming."
(1 John 2:28)

9 798868 500756